# TABLE OF CONTENTS

# *INTRODUCTION*

**M**any females, if they knew how, would probably choose to be ladies. That's why every young female should have a copy of *A Lady by Choice*. This book deserves a preferred place on her nightstand, in her purse, or some other conspicuous place in her life. *A Lady by Choice* is filled with the kind of mannerly teachings that many young ladies today would not ordinarily know – and yet, it is training like this that can take them up society's ladder and into every unique place, from palaces to boardrooms. If read and followed, this book will help improve a young lady's self-esteem and, ultimately, help put her on the road to being the person she's always wanted to be. The truths that author Johnnie Denise Payne puts forth are everlasting, because they are based on a strong grounding in the Word of God. Ruth, Esther, and Mary in the Bible are the kinds of ladies God turns out – women of high self-esteem who make an impact on history and on our lives.

**–The Editors**

*That our daughters
may be as corner stones,
polished after the similitude
of a palace.*

**(Psalm 144:12)**

# *DEDICATION*

This book is dedicated to my lovingly supportive family.

To my husband, Don: your faith in me and support of me appear to have no end. Out of all the girlies in the world, you chose me. How blessed I am!

To my son, Jeremiah, in whom I am well pleased: I thank you for unselfishly sharing me with hundreds of girls over the years.

To my mother, Deloris: I thank you for seeing my appointed path and keeping me on it. You instilled in me the characteristics of a lady by being an example of grace and holiness. I thank you most of all introducing me to Christ at an early age.

To Jaylyn Niccole: I am so excited to see what God has in store for you. You truly are a precious jewel.

To Jackie and Katrina: thank you for your support and encouragement.

**Johnnie**

# *ACKNOWLEDGMENTS*

I acknowledge all the young ladies I have had the privilege of knowing and ministering to over the past twenty-plus years. From those whom I have taught in personal development classes, to those I have counseled, I have benefited at least as much as you. Each of you has imparted so much into my life, and I have learned from all of you.

Remember this: the challenges you go through last only for a season, so never give up; you will make it through.

**Johnnie**

# *This Gift Is Presented*

To _____

On_____

By_____

Dear Young Lady,

It has long been my desire to put this book into your hands. Now that you have it, please thank the thoughtful person who gave it to you on my behalf. As you continue this wonderful journey to becoming the godly young woman you are destined to be, please know that you are never alone. This journey can sometimes seem overwhelming, even frightening, but this is a path that many of us have taken before you, and I'm here to tell you that there are marvelous things in store for the lady by choice.

You are unique and were created with a specific purpose in mind. The fact that you feel, and have always felt different, is because you are different! God designed you for His specific purpose. Don't turn from it, but run to Him.

The world is full of temptations, but you already have inside of you everything you need to overcome any challenge and to accomplish your purpose in the earth. My prayer for you is that you begin to see yourself through God's eyes, and that you never see yourself as less than the precious gem that you are. In God's eyes you have great worth and value.

Lastly, don't waste your talent, and enjoy your journey. I have included my contact information. If you need to be encouraged, I am available and would be honored to help.

Joyfully,
Johnnie D. Payne

# *From*
# *Adolescence*

# *From*
# *Adolescence*

*Dear Young Lady,*

*It has long been my desire to put this book into your hands. Now that you have it, please thank the thoughtful person who gave it to you on my behalf. As you continue this wonderful journey to becoming the godly young woman you are destined to be, please know that you are never alone. This journey can sometimes seem overwhelming, even frightening, but this is a path that many of us have taken before you, and I'm here to tell you that there are marvelous things in store for the lady by choice.*

*You are unique and were created with a specific purpose in mind. The fact that you feel, and have always felt different, is because you are different! God designed you for His specific purpose. Don't turn from it, but run to Him.*

*The world is full of temptations, but you already have inside of you everything you need to overcome any challenge and to accomplish your purpose in the earth. My prayer for you is that you begin to see yourself through God's eyes, and that you never see yourself as less than the precious gem that you are. In God's eyes you have great worth and value.*

*Lastly, don't waste your talent, and enjoy your journey. I have included my contact information. If you need to be encouraged, I am available and would be honored to help.*

*Joyfully,*
*Johnnie D. Payne*

New Collegiate Dictionary is "a woman of refinement and gentle manners." Webster's Encyclopedic Unabridged Dictionary includes the definition: "A woman who is refined, polite, and well-spoken." It also cites the Virgin Mary as an example.

We shouldn't think of a lady as being brainless and mousy, with no option but to bear children and serve men. You'll find ladies in the ministry, government, the corporate world, legal profession, medicine, education, sports, and virtually every field where men are.

What made Mary a lady? The Gospel of Luke offers us a glimpse of her qualities. In Luke 1:27 we see that Mary was a virgin who was betrothed, or promised in marriage, to a man named Joseph. God sent His personal messenger, the angel Gabriel, to her. In verse 28, he said,

*"Hail, thou that art highly favored, the Lord is with thee: blessed art thou among women."*

God's messenger called Mary "highly favored" and

told her she was blessed *"among women."* Mary must have done something right to be set apart from other women. She must have carried herself in some noble way and had some special relationship with God to be called *"highly favored."*

God needed a yielded vessel through which He could bring the Savior into the world. Of all the women available, He found the vessel He was seeking in Mary – the highly favored one. She was probably still in her teens when she married Joseph, since it was customary for Hebrew girls to marry fairly early in life. Mary must have been tremendously honored to be so chosen. God the Father spoke to

her, the Holy Spirit came upon her, and Jesus the Christ came through her. And through it all she remained a virgin because she never defiled herself.

Mary did not draw back from the great assignment God had given to her. In verse 38, she said: ***"Behold the handmaid of the Lord; be it unto me according to thy word."*** She must have been very brave on top of everything else.

One thing is certain – Mary was a true lady.

How would you describe a lady? Does your description agree with the following list?

At the outset we see three characteristics that Mary possessed: Mary was highly favored and blessed among women. The Amplified Bible says, *"Blessed – favored of God – are you before all other women!"* She was also a virgin, which means she kept herself pure from sexual sin.

❒ A lady will not dress in a manner that is too revealing. (In other words, she will not wear clothes that are too short, too tight, or too low-cut).

❒ A lady will not participate in gossip.

❒ A lady always practices common courtesy.

❒ A lady does not allow young men to kiss and pet her body because she realizes she is special.

❏ A lady does not use profanity.
(She realizes that her mouth is clean).

❏ A lady practices good hygiene.

❏ A lady is not loud or obnoxious
in public.

❏ A lady does not hold grudges against
others.

❏ A lady will do all she can to help
her family run smoothly.

❏ A lady is careful about the kind of
music she listens to.

❏ A lady can be trusted with secrets.

❏ A lady chooses to be a peacemaker
instead of a mess-starter.

❏ A lady knows how to give and
receive compliments.

❏ A lady practices good table manners.

❏ A lady shows proper respect for
those in authority.

❐ A lady knows when to speak and when to be quiet.

❐ A lady is a good sport.

❐ A lady will not tell jokes at the expense of others.

❐ A lady will not fight if she can help it.

# *Points to Remember*

**1.** Anything that has the ability to reproduce is considered a female, but not every female is a lady.

**2.** Doors of opportunity open for ladies that do not open for the average female.

**3.** Webster's Dictionary cites Mary as an example of a lady.

**4.** Mary's life demonstrated these three characteristics: she was highly favored of the Lord, she was blessed among women, and she was a virgin.

**5.** Mary did not draw back from the great assignment God had given her.

**6.** Choosing to be a lady does not mean you are brainless and mousy, with no option but to bear children and serve men.

*...that our daughters may be as corner stones, polished after the similitude of a palace.* *(Psalm 144:12)*

*NOTES*

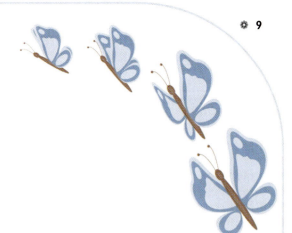

## Chapter 2

# *Feminine Hygiene*

*I*t is important for a young lady to develop the practice of good hygiene. A lady who practices good hygiene sets the first standard for achievement in life.

There is something very special and pleasing about a female who has a pleasant smell, has clean hair, has fresh breath and wears clean clothes.

You may have many God-given gifts and talents, but if you do not practice good hygiene, you won't be accepted in social situations. Others will look upon you as being

lazy, untrained, and undisciplined. It will be difficult for others to take you seriously if you do not keep your body, as well your clothes, clean and neat.

This cuts across economic lines. Even a young lady who is raised in a family with a limited income can bathe, take care of her teeth and hair and wash her clothes on a regular basis. This is the most basic area of femininity for any young lady who is concerned about being the best she can be.

### *Keeping Your Temple Clean*

The female body is very different from the male body because of its ability to reproduce. The parts of the female body that are used in reproduction go through a regular monthly cycle called menstruation. Failure to care properly for the body during this important time is the most common reason for poor hygiene in young ladies.

If the vagina is not kept clean, it will emit a foul, musty odor that is impossible to cover up, and this can be very embarrassing. It is a telltale sign to those who may come in contact with such a female that she does not properly care for her private parts.

Warm showers are heavenly. I truly thank God for the person who invented the showerhead. How fortunate we are to live in a country with free-flowing water piped into our homes. So many young ladies in other countries do not have this basic luxury.

To cleanse your body, start with the water as warm as

you can stand it. Let it completely soak your entire body for several minutes before adding soap. Your pores will open in response to the warm water, and the cleansing process will begin immediately.

After a few minutes, using a cotton washcloth or loofah, add soap. Gently scrub your entire body before rinsing with warm water. Rinse several times until the water runs clear. Be sure to rinse your private areas thoroughly to remove all soap.

I suggest a shower in the morning and a bath at night. In the morning a warm shower will wash away all the sweat and dead skin cells your body has sloughed off during the night, which is when the body does its own natural cleansing.

A warm bath at night (with bubbles, of course) will help you relax and prepare you for a good night's sleep.

Remember: THE HABITS YOU FORM AS A TEENAGER – BOTH GOOD AND BAD – WILL SET THE PATTERN FOR YOUR LATER LIFE.

Did you know that you can smell bad and not know it? It's true. We are so familiar with our own body odors that we may not be aware of how we smell to others. By the time we become aware of our smell, others have already gotten a whiff of our body odor.

It is a good idea to mark your calendar each month to determine when your period begins and ends. This will help you to be prepared for any "surprises." You should carry a panty liner (a small feminine pad) in your purse a few days before your cycle is scheduled to start. In this way you will not risk staining your underwear and having to keep it on in school all day. If you are not prepared when your cycle begins, others may know it. The blood your cycle eliminates is a waste product, and it carries an odor with it that is strong and distinctive.

Although all females are made the same, our bodies function differently. Your cycle may last seven days, whereas your girlfriend's may last five days. In order to practice good hygiene, it is necessary to pay attention to the way your own body functions.

Too much hair under the arms is unsightly and will cause heavy sweating. Some young ladies shave their underarms, while others use hair removal creams like Neet or Nair. Never try removing any body hair without a parent's permission and instruction, however. When your parent or guardian feels that you are ready, they will help you select the method and products that are best for you.

### *Clean Underclothes*

Wearing unclean underclothes contributes to poor hygiene. While teaching a class on hygiene at a local middle school, I asked a group of young ladies how often they change their underclothes. Several of them said they only change their bras once or twice a week. Although only a few spoke up, I'm sure there were others who did the same.

Many young ladies believe it is all right to wear underclothes several days in a row without changing them because they are hidden and they think no one can tell if they are not clean. Underclothes are the closest garments to your body and they have a "language" of their own. They absorb per-spiration, body odors, and discharges first. The fact that others cannot see your underclothes does not mean they cannot smell them.

The most important reason for practicing good hygiene, however, is you. Cleanliness can become a health issue, and is most definitely a self-esteem issue.

The decision is yours. Will you be known as a young lady who keeps her temple clean? This is certainly one way in which you can bring glory to your heavenly Father, and feel good about yourself while doing so.

## *Proper Care of the Teeth and Mouth*

Proper care of the teeth and mouth is important for good hygiene. Keeping your mouth clean requires extra care and attention. Be sure to include regular flossing to help get rid of food caught between the teeth close to the gum area.

It is a good idea to carry a breath freshener in your purse or a small bottle of mouthwash. When brushing your teeth, be sure to brush your tongue also. The tongue is a breeding ground for odors that may lead to bad breath. You will imme-diately notice how fresh your mouth feels after brushing your tongue as well as your teeth.

I have listed a few products that can be purchased to help keep your body clean and fresh. The products will only help you, however, if you start out with a clean body. To use perfumes, powders, deodorants, and other hygiene aids on your body without washing it first will not give you good results. You cannot cover up bad body odor resulting from poor hygiene. Before you use any of the following aids, start with a warm shower or bath, using good soap or body wash.

## *Products to Aid in Feminine Hygiene*

Pantiliners
Sanitary pads
Deodorant soaps
Perfumes
Hair remover creams

Sachets
(small pouch of perfumed powder for your drawers and closets)

Lotions
Underarm deodorants
Mouthwash
Dental floss
Shampoo and conditioner

Now it is time for you to put the things you've learned in this chapter into practice. Your body requires extra care and attention, because God created you with a special purpose in mind. Treat your body as His special creation. Take time to pamper yourself, and always take good care of God's temple.

# Points to Remember

**1.** Keeping your body and clothes clean and neat is the most basic area of femininity.

**2.** Failure to care properly for your body during menstruation is the most common reason for poor hygiene.

**3.** We become so familiar with our own body odors that we may not be aware of how we smell to others.

**4.** In order to practice good hygiene, it is necessary to pay attention to the way your body functions.

**5.** Never try removing any body hair without your parents' permission and instruction.

**6.** Proper care of your teeth and mouth is important for good hygiene.

***For God hath not called us unto uncleanness, but unto holiness.***
*(1 Thessalonians 4:7)*

*NOTES*

## Chapter 3

# *Understanding Your Body*

*A*s I've shared the principles in this book with young ladies over the past several years, I've come to the conclusion that most do not know or understand how their bodies function. When some young ladies begin to menstruate, for example, they become frightened and fearful.

*Christie was eleven years old when her menstrual cycle began. At school one Friday afternoon, she felt a little wetness in her panties. This was very unusual for her, so she headed to the restroom. Before she could get there, she began discharging heavily. Blood flowed down her legs. When she saw it, she began screaming to those around her that she was dying, and she begged them to help her. This experience was very traumatic for Christie. However, this trauma could have been avoided if she had been told in advance that it was perfectly normal in her family for young ladies to begin menstruating at about eleven years of age, and that her mother and older sister had begun their cycles with heavy flows, as well.*

Family genetics play a big role in female bodily functions. Christie could have been prepared for this experience had she been better educated about what to expect. The school nurse discussed this very special change that was taking place in her body with Christie, who told the nurse that she knew her period would start, but she did not know there could be so much blood without something being wrong. The book on menstruation her mother had given her to read earlier that year had not prepared her for what happened when her first period began.

When a young lady understands the changes her body undergoes during adolescence, the adjustments she has to make will not seem as frightening or difficult as they might have otherwise.

## *Development of the Female Adolescent*

When a young lady reaches puberty, which is the physical change from girl to woman that usually begins around age eleven, her body will produce a hormone called estrogen. This hormone is responsible for storing fat. It also determines how heavy and how long her monthly cycle will be. Estrogen also keeps her skin smooth, her bones hard, and her body tissues soft. The female body stops pro-ducing estrogen around the age of fifty.

Similarly, the male body will begin to produce the hormone testosterone during puberty. Male puberty usual-ly begins around the age of fourteen. Testosterone is responsible for muscle development and for hair growth on the face and body. It is during this time that the young

man's voice changes. The male hormone testosterone is also responsible for burning body fat in young men. Don't you think it is interesting that the female hormone estrogen promotes the storage of fat and the male hormone testos-terone does the exact opposite? God wanted males and females not only to look different from each other but to be different, as well. But in their differences they complement one another.

Females will gain most of their height during ages eleven to thirteen, while males will continue to grow until they reach sixteen or seventeen.

During the ages of thirteen to eighteen, the female will gain an average of forty pounds. The reason for this is

that the female body during adolescence is dedicated to storing fat in preparation for childbearing. However, this is not to say that a teen-age lady is ready to become a parent. It is simply that her body is being prepared to function as a woman instead of a girl. This is one of the most important changes every female will undergo during her lifetime.

Body image is basically the way a person feels about his or her body, regardless of the way he or she looks. The body image of a young lady will often affect her entire personality.

A lot of teen-age ladies do not like their bodies. If you fall into this category, you are not alone. An unbelievable number of adult women do not like their bodies either. This is the reason so many women are having cosmetic surgery today. Teen-age ladies are having their noses changed and their thighs and hips liposuctioned in large numbers. There is a lot of pressure on females to look like the women who seem to have perfect bodies, women we see in magazines, on videos, on television, and in movies. What many teen-agers do not realize is that the pictures in the magazines have often been altered to make the models appear perfect. This idea of perfection may differ from person to person. Therefore, we need to ask, according to whose standard should perfection be measured?

God made each of us unique. He knew exactly what He was doing when He created you and me, because He created us as a complement to someone who would appreciate the way we're constructed. Ladies with "fine" bodies may turn a guy's head, but many of those same guys won't look only for a stunning body when they are ready to marry. They will look for the person who complements them most.

God designed our facial features – lips, eyes, nose and ears – exactly the way He wanted them to be. Our height, skin color, hair texture – whether curly, kinky or straight – was all planned by the Master Creator. It was no accident. When the heavenly Father created you and me, He did so with a particular purpose in mind. Everything about us fits into God's purpose for our lives. To look at yourself as somehow being a mistake is to slap your Maker in the face.

To overcome a poor body image, you must believe that God made you just the way He wanted you to be. And remember, He makes no mistakes. If there are areas you can improve on, then do so. If you are not pleased with your hair, for instance, because it appears dry or unhealthy, try deep conditioning twice a month. Curling irons and straightening combs may cause the ends of your hair to become damaged, so it might be helpful to limit their use. Perming, bleaching, and coloring have also been known to cause damage. A good haircut and a regular trim along with regular conditioning can take your hair from damaged to lovely.

Ask God to show you what to do about your area of concern. He will give you the answers you need. If it is important to you, it is important to Him. He wants you to talk to Him about everything in your life. When He gives you the answers, don't forget to thank Him!

Your teen-age years are too important to spend shrinking from all that life has to offer because of a poor body image. Work on the things you have the ability to improve. Guard against being unrealistic about having to obtain "the perfect body" according to the world's standards. Remember, you are perfect for His purpose just as you are right now!

# *Points to Remember*

**1.** Family genetics play a big role in female bodily functions.

**2.** When a young lady reaches puberty, her body will produce a hormone called estrogen.

**3.** Estrogen is responsible for storing fat.

**4.** Everything about you fits into God's purpose for your life.

**5.** To overcome a poor body image, you must believe that God made you just the way He wanted you to be.

**6.** Everything that is important to you is important to God.

*I will praise thee; for I am fearfully and wonderfully made: marvelous are thy works; and that my soul knoweth right well.*

*(Psalm 139:14)*

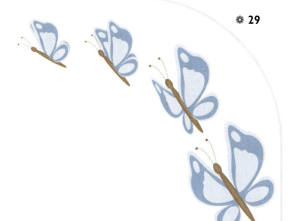

*NOTES*

**Chapter 4**

# *Controlling Your Weight*

*A*re you concerned about your weight? If you aren't right now, chances are you will be at some point in the future. Diet-related illnesses are more common than you may know. This is the major reason why it is so important to develop good habits of exercise and healthy eating.

Weight control is not the easiest goal to accomplish. It takes hard work and discipline. In order to achieve this goal you will need to include large amounts of fresh fruits and vegetables in your diet, as well as limit your intake of fried foods and sweets. And you should seriously consider a good exercise plan, as well.

Listed below are some of the reasons why women become overweight and the effects a poor diet and the lack of exercise have on the body.

A person becomes overweight by eating more food than their body burns off. Body fat is simply unused stored energy.

***One of the most common reasons for being overweight is heredity.*** There is a forty percent chance that you will be overweight if one of your parents is overweight. If both of your parents are overweight, your chances jump to eighty percent. If neither parent is overweight, your chances drop to ten percent.

Fat cells are passed on through your genes. Just as you inherit your eye color, hair texture, and other features from your parents, you may have also inherited their fat cells. The job of a fat cell is to store fat. This explains why females in the same family are usually built the same way. More often than not, your mother's problem areas – such as hips, thighs, and upper arms may become a similar challenge for you.

***Some people are overweight because of environment.*** These persons usually come from food-oriented families. When a family is food-oriented, every gathering or social event is centered around large amounts of food. Often such families have Sunday dinners with heavy, fatty dishes.

Food-oriented families usually have members who are excellent cooks. This knowledge is passed down from one generation to the next. Special recipes and methods of cooking in such families are regarded as being almost sacred. This was certainly the case in my family. My mother and two of my aunts are excellent cooks. Food was pre-

pared days in advance for every holiday and special occasion. This food would include homemade ice cream, cakes,
rolls, turkeys, hams, fried chicken, pies, and cobblers.

I love to cook. Even as a little girl I would hang out in
the kitchen watching my aunts, Marion and Helen, and my
mother, Deloris, prepare food for birthdays and holidays.

I would not trade those times with the women in my
family for anything. The conversations we shared during
the preparation of meals taught me so much about being
a woman, mother, and wife. Those sessions in the kitchen
with my mom and aunts also taught me how to work as a
member of a team in pursuit of a common goal. Each
woman had her own particular strengths and was eager to
bring them to the table to assure that each meal would be
complete and enjoyable.

My Aunt Marion loves to try new recipes for holiday
get-togethers, and she has a knack for presenting food in a
most appealing manner. My mom and Aunt Helen prepare
meats, vegetables and desserts that are so inviting that the
aroma will almost lift you up and float you into the kitchen
for a pinch of roast, a taste of greens, or a hot roll dripping
with butter. I love the look on the faces of these godly
women as our family gathers around the table to enjoy
their labors of love.

My challenge, however, has been to learn healthier ways of preparing food. I have had to learn to cut down on fat intake and prepare smaller amounts of food instead of cooking as though an army was coming to dinner.

Our environment, methods of preparing foods, and the eating habits we form as children can certainly contribute to weight problems.

***Stress is another common reason for being overweight.*** Your own personal stress or stress within the family may tempt you to "eat away" your problems instead of facing them. Females especially are known to use food to "stuff" their feelings of loneliness, rejection, fear, and procrastination. At such times we do not need to be hungry to eat. Food becomes a diversion, something to do instead of facing the challenges that are before us.

Challenges are a part of life. For those of us who have a relationship with Jesus Christ, our solution is to turn to Him for the answers we need instead of using food to fill the void.

There is no one who loves us more and encourages us more than Jesus. He wants us to come through the challenges in life as winners. Take time to open your Bible to find out what God says about the challenges you are facing. For example, 1 Corinthians 10:13 says:

***"There hath no temptation taken you but such as is common to man; but God is faithful, who will not suffer you to be tempted above that ye are able; but will with the temptation also make the way of escape, that ye may be able to bear it."***

In other words, the struggles you may be having with controlling your diet are not unique. Millions go through the same thing, but with God you can handle the temptations and not yield to them.

When we use food to ease our pain during stressful periods, we may develop habits that are not only hard to break but do physical damage to our bodies, as well. When we are tempted to stress-eat, we do not usually reach for carrot sticks or apples. We usually reach for foods with high amounts of sugar and starch. Handling problems this way eventually leads to a low self-image and excessive weight gain. Stress-eating has no long-term benefits and leads to many unwanted pounds.

***Food choices can be another cause of being over-weight.*** Some recent surveys indicate that teen-age young ladies take in the least nutritious food of any age group or gender. In a lot of homes, when a young lady becomes a teen-ager she is allowed to eat whatever she wants. More often than not she will choose fast food and candy. Both are loaded with fats and calories.

Being overweight is only one result of a poor diet. There are many diseases that result from poor nutrition and a lack of exercise. Some of the most common diseases are diabetes, heart disease, hypertension, obesity, and cancer.

Change is possible, but to change unhealthy eating habits will take dedication, determination, and consistency. Care enough about yourself to assure yourself a healthy future, one that is free of sickness and disease. Choose a life-style of regular exercise and a diet that will aid your body and not destroy it.

### Try Counting Calories

Do you know what is in the food you eat? Many people don't, and most don't care. Learning to read food labels is very simple and can be very informative. You would probably be surprised to know how much sugar and fat are in the foods you eat daily. By law, ingredients and their amounts must be listed on all food packaging.

For instance, the Snickers bar is advertised as packed with peanuts and offering quick energy. A regular size bar is 2.07 ounces. Listed on the package are these nutritional facts:

Calories 280

Fat total 14 grams

Sugars 29 grams

### A Word About Fats and Sugar

Although fats like butter and mayonnaise add flavor to the foods we enjoy, they also add a lot of calories. There are approximately nine calories in each gram of fat. Excess fat in your body can clog your arteries and cause excessive weight gain.

Sugar makes many nutritious foods more pleasing to the taste. The sugar you sprinkle on your morning oatmeal and the syrup that tops your Saturday morning pancakes should only be used moderately. White sugar has about fifteen calories per teaspoon.

Ingredients are listed for food packaging in the order of the amount in the food. The first two ingredients listed on the Snickers bar are milk chocolate and sugar. This means that there is more milk chocolate than sugar in the candy bar, and more sugar than the next ingredients listed, cocoa butter and milk.

Take time to read the labels on food items before you consume them. Get out of the habit of eating something just because it tastes good. Although it may taste good, it may not be good for you. You may decide after reading the label of a Snickers bar, for instance, that you do not want to consume twenty-nine grams of sugar, and 280 calories in a single candy bar.

On the following pages there are a list of popular fast-food items and the number of calories they contain. Pick your favorites and add up the number of calories you would consume after attending a school game or social event in which you snacked on these items. Remember, 3,500 calories can put a pound of weight on you. The recommended caloric intake for females is 2,500 a day. Most of us go over that suggested number of calories in the snacks we eat daily.

Make a decision today to commit to a regular exercise program. Remember, it's time to develop good habits that will carry on into your adult life. Regular exercise should be a part of both your present and future life-style. The decision is yours. What will it be for you – swimming, bicycling, running, or working out with weights? You decide the activity. Be consistent and reap the benefits of a beautiful, healthy body and a sharp, clear mind.

### Exercising to Stay Fit

Did you know that the Lord wants you to be in the best physical shape possible?

| SUBWAY | CALORIES | FAT GRAMS |
|---|---|---|
| 6" Veggie Delite | 232 | 3 |
| 6" Classic Italian B. L.T. | 450 | 21 |
| 6" Cold Cut Trio | 374 | 14 |
| 6" Ham | 293 | 5 |
| 6" Roast Beef | 296 | 5 |
| 6" Subway Club | 304 | 5 |
| 6" Turkey | 282 | 4 |
| 6" Tuna w/light mayo | 378 | 14 |
| 6" Meatball | 413 | 15 |

| BURGER KING | CALORIES | FAT GRAMS |
|---|---|---|
| Whopper | 630 | 38 |
| Whopper w/cheese | 720 | 46 |
| Double Whopper | 920 | 59 |
| Bacon Double Cheeseburger | 620 | 28 |
| Bacon Cheeseburger | 400 | 22 |
| BK Broiler Fish Filet | 720 | 43 |
| BK Chicken Sandwich | 710 | 26 |
| Chicken Tenders | 236 | 13 |
| Chef salad with out dressing | 178 | 9 |
| French Fries-small | 250 | 13 |
| Onion Rings | 380 | 19 |
| Chocolate Shake | 440 | 10 |
| Vanilla Shake | 430 | 9 |

| DOMINO'S PIZZA | CALORIES | FAT GRAMS |
|---|---|---|
| 12" Classic Hand Tossed | | |
| Cheese 2 slices | 375 | 11 |
| Pepperoni 2 slices | 448 | 18 |
| Veggie 2 slices | 391 | 12 |
| 12" Thin Crust | | |
| Cheese 2 slices | 273 | 12 |
| Pepperoni 2 slices | 347 | 18 |
| Veggie 2 slices | 289 | 13 |

| McDONALD'S | CALORIES | FAT GRAMS |
| --- | --- | --- |
| Hamburger | 270 | 9 |
| Cheeseburger | 320 | 13 |
| Quarter Pounder with cheese | 530 | 30 |
| Big Mac | 570 | 32 |
| Filet O Fish | 470 | 26 |
| French Fries Small | 210 | 10 |
| French Fries Super Size | 610 | 29 |
| Chicken McNuggets 6 pieces | 290 | 17 |
| Vanilla Cone | 150 | 4.5 |
| Hot Fudge Sundae | 340 | 12 |
| Oreo McFlurry | 570 | 20 |
| McDonaldland Cookies | 180 | 5 |
| Vanilla Shake - small | 360 | 9 |

| TACO BELL | CALORIES | FAT GRAMS |
| --- | --- | --- |
| Bean Burrito | 370 | 12 |
| Burrito Supreme Beef | 520 | 22 |
| Burrito Supreme Chicken | 430 | 18 |
| Zesty Chicken Border Bowl | 460 | 19 |
| Tostada | 250 | 12 |
| Mexican Pizza | 540 | 35 |
| Cheese Quesadilla | 490 | 28 |
| Nachos | 320 | 18 |
| Nachos Supreme | 440 | 24 |
| Taco Salad with Salsa | 210 | 12 |
| Soft Chicken Taco | 190 | 7 |
| Soft Beef Taco | 210 | 10 |

| CARL'S JR. | CALORIES | FAT GRAMS |
|---|---|---|
| Famous Star Burger | 580 | 32 |
| Super Star Hamburger | 790 | 45 |
| Western Bacon Cheeseburger | 650 | 30 |
| Double Western Bacon Cheeseburger | 900 | 49 |
| Charbroiled BBQ Chicken Sandwich | 280 | 3 |
| Charbroiled Santa Fe | | |
| Chicken Sandwich | 510 | 31 |
| Carl's Catch Fish Sandwich | 510 | 27 |
| Garden Salad to go | 50 | 2.5 |
| French Fries regular order | 290 | 14 |
| Onion Rings | 430 | 21 |
| Chocolate Shake Small | 390 | 7 |
| Vanilla Shake-Small | 330 | 8 |

The Lord wants to use young people to draw others to Him. Your body makes a statement to others about who you are and how you feel about yourself. Ask yourself what statement does your body make? Does it show that you care for the temple God has given you? If not, start paying more attention to your temple and give it the exercise it requires.

Exercising should be fun. I believe the only way you will exercise regularly is by finding out what form of exercise you truly enjoy. Perhaps you like taking long walks, skating, or playing tennis. Maybe you like to jog or ski, play softball or basketball, or swim, golf or hike. The key is to decide what you like and determine to work it into your day. Being consistent makes all the difference. To benefit most from exercise, you must do it at least four days a week, thirty to forty-five minutes each time. It usually takes about six weeks to see definite improvement from exercise. However, you will feel better immediately.

You may feel sore for a couple of days because you are stretching muscles beyond their usual comfortable limits, but the soreness goes away after a few days.

Regular exercise is a very important part of controlling your weight. Several young ladies have told me that they do not exercise regularly apart from what is required of them in their physical education classes because they believe only those who are overweight should exercise. This is not true. Although exercising on a regular basis can help control your weight, there are many other benefits to be derived from it, as well. Let's look at a few of them.

## *Benefits of Exercising*

❒ It helps reduce stress and tension. You will be better able to think things through. There is something wonderful that happens in your brain when you exert physical energy.

❏   It increases metabolism.  Metabolism is the rate at which your body burns fat.

❏   It helps heighten your self-esteem. You will swell with pride as you see your body become firm, and the pounds and inches fall off.

❏   It aids blood circulation. This is great for both your skin and your heart.

❏   It increases your energy level.  You will be better able to do the things your day requires without becoming tired as quickly.  Endurance is a valuable benefit of exercise.

# *My Commitment to Exercise*

I _____

make a promise to myself to exercise on a

regular basis – at least four times a week.

The forms of exercise I choose are

_____    _____    _____

Date:

_____

Signed by

_____

# *Points to Remember*

**1.** Body fat is simply unused, stored energy.

**2.** Just as you inherit your eye color, hair texture, and other features from your parents, you may have also inherited their fat cells.

**3.** Personal stress or stress within the family may tempt you to "eat away" your problems instead of facing them.

**4.** Some recent surveys indicate that teen-age ladies take in the least nutritious food of any age group or gender.

**5.** Diabetes, heart disease, hypertension, obesity, and cancer may result from poor nutrition and lack of exercise.

**6.** The Lord wants you to be in the best physical shape possible.

*...To him that overcometh will I give to eat of the tree of life, which is in the midst of the paradise of God.* (Revelation 2:7)

*NOTES*

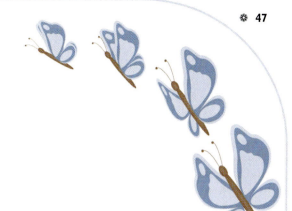

## Chapter 5

# *Eating Disorders*

*M*ore young ladies than ever are literally dying for "that perfect body." They are so concerned about how they look that they risk ruining their health through a binge-and-purge cycle and engaging in other eating disorders. These patterns of eating cause behaviors that affect a person in many unhealthy ways, both physically and emotionally.

Food is necessary to sustain our physical bodies. Because it is so necessary, it is easy to abuse. There are no laws that regulate how much or how little a person should eat. However, the effects of an eating disorder are often life-threatening.

Food becomes a problem for us when we use it as a substitute for friendship, love, or success, or when we deny ourselves a proper diet.

Most problems or challenges that cause eating disorders are the result of major changes in one's family or life-style, such as a family move, breaking up with a boyfriend, parents getting divorced or remarried, and the death of a close friend or relative. They can also be caused by school or social pressures such as competition (sports, gymnastics, academics), decisions about college, wanting to be popular, wanting to be liked by boys, and grades.

Anorexia nervosa is considered the most serious of all eating disorders. Anorexia is described as an abnormal fear of becoming fat. About ten to fifteen percent of the victims of anorexia die from the disease. Anorexia was once a rare disease, affecting only a few people, and many of them were wealthy.

In the past twenty-five years, anorexia nervosa has increased among junior and senior high school students. Every year about 3,750 or more deaths are attributed to this eating disorder.

Most victims of anorexia are between the ages of eleven and twenty, and it is ten times more common in girls than in boys.

Many anorexics are from middle-class or wealthy homes where material possessions are easily available to them. Although a variety of food is typically available in large amounts in their homes, the anorexic will consistently refuse to eat.

A young lady suffering from anorexia may appear to be "perfect," and may be known for giving her parents and teachers very few problems. But it is possible that she has become "the model of perfection" to make up for something lacking in her home life. This facade breaks down when she becomes a teen-ager. The teen years are years when she must face the changes occurring in her body, as well as deal with the uncertainties that come as a result of developing into a young woman.

I know a young woman named Keisha, who is now a wife and a mother. She once suffered from anorexia. Keisha is very charming and talented and has a wonderful husband and a beautiful, six-year-old son. But Keisha is still haunted by anorexia nervosa, which began when she was sixteen years old and lasted for eleven years.

## Keisha's Story

*During my early teen years my body began to change from that of a girl to that of a woman. I began to develop hips and breasts. Until then, I had always been considered skinny. I was having a very hard time handling the changes in my body. The attention I was receiving from men scared me, and I felt awkward and unsure of how to handle it. I began to look different in my clothes, and developments that should have filled me with pride shocked and repelled me. It was too much too soon.*

*In what seemed to me a very short period of time, I went from 100 pounds to more than 120 pounds. When I looked in the mirror, all I saw was fat looking back at me. It filled me with fear and panic.*

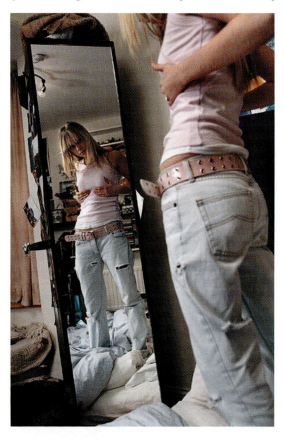

*I would hardly eat anything. Day after day, as I went through a routine of school and after-school activities, I ate as little as possible. Sometimes my stomach would burn so badly that it felt like it was on fire. At times I would become lightheaded. My ribs and bones stuck out, and yet I loved to feel hungry. The more I starved myself, the thinner I got. I could go for days without eating. Still, I looked in the mirror and appeared fat. I saw fat on my arms, stomach and thighs.*

### *Keisha Didn't Reach the Critical Point*

Keisha's weight leveled off before it reached a critical point. This sometimes happens to anorexics. They reach a point where they are not able to lose weight in large amounts. Keisha was very fortunate, as well.

There were two very special people in her life who prayed for her, her mom and her best friend, Nikki. Every night

she and Nikki would pray together over the telephone, asking that God would be glorified in Keisha's life since Keisha had received Christ as her Lord and Savior when she was nine years old.

Nikki reminded the Lord of the time when she and Keisha attended summer camp in the mountains. At the evening fireside rally on their last night there, the message was about what it meant to allow Jesus to be Lord of your life. Though Keisha and Nikki were very young, in their hearts they knew they were hearing the truth.

Nikki reminded God that her friend Keisha had made Him Lord of her life on that warm summer night more than seven years before, and that anorexia, therefore, had no claim on her. God did intervene, and Keisha went on to establish a normal life. But there are hundreds of young ladies who are not as fortunate as she was. Some struggle with anorexia nervosa for years and many even lose their lives to it.

How would you know if you or someone you know were headed for trouble in this area? Let's look at a few of the signs that may appear in the life of someone with anorexia nervosa:

❐ She may pull away from friends and loved ones.

❐ She may become rude and noncommunicative.

❐ She may withdraw from most activities.

❐ She may stop having her menstrual cycle.

❐ She may have restless energy.

❐ She will see her emaciated body as being fat.

❐ She will hide food to keep from eating it.

❐ She may use laxatives regularly.

❒ She may be very sensitive to cold weather.

❒ She may exercise constantly.

❒ She may have infections or sores that will not heal.

❒ She may have dry, patchy hair.

❒ She may have yellowish or dulllooking skin.

❒ She may have the most obvious sign of all, extreme weight loss.

It is critical for anyone who is suffering from anorexia to get help as soon as possible. The sooner they get help, the better their chance of complete recovery will be. Anorexia nervosa is curable, although the person suffering from it may have to be hospitalized and force-fed for a while. In such cases a tube may be inserted into the major artery above the heart to allow liquid nourishment to flow into the stomach. This method of force-feeding allows the patient to regain weight quickly.

Another method of force-feeding is by inserting a feeding tube through the anorexic's throat. The problem with this method is that many anorexics can and do force themselves to throw up after they are fed in this manner.

A vital part of the anorexic's recovery is counseling, which is necessary to determine the underlying reasons for the disorder. Such counseling works best when the entire family is involved.

## Bulimia: The Act of Purging

Bulimics devour large amounts of food and then purge their bodies of it with laxatives or by vomiting. Unlike the

anorexic, who refuses to eat, the bulimic binges on from 1,000 to 20,000 calories at a time.

Usually most of the foods she chooses are sweets and starches. Bulimics who are in treatment say that most of their thoughts are about food. They are constantly thinking about what to have for breakfast, lunch, and dinner.

Bulimia is considered a social illness, rooted in what society says a person should look like. Girl's schools are breeding grounds for bulimics, and their students often teach each other how to purge after they have binged.

Actress Jane Fonda writes about her struggle with bulimia in her best-selling book, *Jane Fonda's Workout Book*. She tells how she began to binge and purge in school. She continued this behavior through most of her teen-age years. Today she relies on exercise and healthy eating to stay in shape. Jane Fonda is a beautiful example of what exercise and healthy eating can do.

Bulimics often talk about a deep emotional hunger that comes over them suddenly. They hope that by stuffing themselves with food they will feel better and lose the empty feeling

they have deep inside. But most of the time their problems are too deep to easily recognize and too overwhelming to face without help. To the bulimic food means comfort, warmth, and security.

Some bulimics say their problems started when a strict diet regimen they were on failed. Often, bulimics will take large amounts of diet pills and laxatives.

Constant vomiting can cause the blood vessels in the eyes to break. The gases in the stomach that break food down can erode the enamel off one's teeth when the contents of the stomach are constantly brought up to the mouth through vomiting. In some cases, frequent vomiting may even cause the esophagus to rupture, and this may lead to death.

Bulimics may have irregular menstrual cycles, or they may stop menstruating completely. Dizziness, cramps, and extreme tiredness may also be the result of their binge-and-purge cycles.

## *Important to Ask for Help*

Asking for help is a difficult step for the bulimic, but it is also a most important one. Bulimia is such a secret disorder that often a person must be caught and reported in order to receive the help she needs. For a bulimic to ask for help is to admit there is a problem and that it is out of control. When discovered, it is necessary for the bulimic to be completely honest about the length of time and frequency of the purging that has taken place.

Bulimia is curable, but it usually involves either individual or group counseling . It is important for the bulimic to feel comfortable and develop complete trust in the therapist and other group members. There are several treatment clinics *(see listing on pages 180-184)* that require the patient to stay for long periods. Many of them are effective in helping bulimics face their problems. A very important part of their total recovery is a thorough physical examination by a doctor who specializes in internal medicine – an internist.

The bulimic needs to work primarily in two areas for recovery – the psychological and the physical. Psychological help enables her to explore her feelings regarding family and childhood in order to find the root of her eating disorder. Our heavenly Father also deals with the disorders (sin) in our lives from the root. As in gardening, where we often have to dig deep to loosen the dirt around the root of a weed before we can pull it out, so it is with bulimia.  Once the root is out, however, the weed is gone forever. If we only deal with the symptoms, which are the behavior that can be seen on the surface, we won't be effective. Treating the symptoms does not allow us to deal with the true problem, whether it is an eating disorder or something else that has kept us from being all God intends us to be.

❏ Up to five percent of all American women are bulimics.

❏ The ratio of women to men with eating disorders is ten to one.

❏ About half of those suffering from anorexia have been or are bulimic.

❏ In one study, bulimics saw themselves as 80.6 percent larger than they were. Anorexic women perceived their bodies to be 73.6 percent larger than they were.

❏ The typical bulimic comes from a middle-to-upper-class family.  Her father is likely to work in such professions as medicine, law, or education.

❏ Young ladies suffering from anorexia or bulimia are usually perfectionists or high-achievers.

❏ One or more of the bulimic's parents could also have a problem with food.

❏ There may be a family history of chemical dependency or depression.

# Points to Remember

**1.** Most problems or challenges that cause eating disorders are the result of major changes in the family or one's life-style.

**2.** Anorexia is described as an abnormal fear of becoming fat.

**3.** Anorexics often seem to be a picture of "the perfect young lady."

**4.** Bulimia involves devouring large amounts of food followed by purging.

**5.** Bulimics say most of their thoughts are about food.

**6.** To a bulimic, food means comfort, warmth, and security.

**He healeth the broken in heart, and bindeth up their wounds.**

*(Psalm 147:3)*

*Disclaimer:*

*I am neither a medical doctor nor a health practioner. The information I have provided has been pulled from various sources that I have researched over the years. It is merely meant as a guide to assist you on the road to greater awareness of possible health challenges. If you suspect that you might have a medical problem, see your health care provider.*

*- Johnnie Payne*

*NOTES*

**Chapter 6**

# *Your*
# *Self-Esteem*

*W*hat is self-esteem? Simply stated, it is the value you place on yourself and the opinion you have of yourself.

Your self-esteem is developed from the way you think others see you. The "others" are those who are or have been primary figures in your life–parents, guardians, close relatives and, in some cases, teachers.

These are the people we usually trust to tell us the truth, either by what they say or fail to say, or how we interpret their treatment of us. Often, the absence of a parent through separation, divorce, or death may send the message, though it may be unintentional, that we are not worthy of love.

If you have been told positive things and given affection and attention most of your life, chances are you have a healthy self-image. If the opposite is true, and you have not received these positive things chances are your sense of self-esteem needs to be adjusted.

### *Identifying Low Self-esteem*

A young lady with low self-esteem may be shy and quiet because she has received a lot of criticism in her life. As a result, she may find it difficult to comment or give her opinion during discussions or conversations.

However, there are other young ladies with low self-esteem who are outgoing and may have personalities that make them the life of the party. Such young ladies may dress in ways that are revealing, and may even be promiscuous in relationships with young men. It is very likely, in such a case, that these young ladies are reaching out for the love and acceptance they did not receive in their early years from the primary people in their lives.

It is so important not to judge others based on what we see. Usually, if a young lady's behavior is unfavorable, it is because she is hurting inside. We should always try to look past what appears on the surface. God looks at the heart of a person, and we should endeavor to do so, too.

Some young ladies have experienced verbal abuse in their homes. One young lady I worked with told me that she would rather be hit by her mother than to have her say abusive things to her.

Hitting is not okay, but verbal abuse has devastating

effects on a person's self-esteem. The abusive words and put-downs play over and over again in our minds like a tape recording. The tape continually plays all the abusive things that were ever said to us. Can you imagine hearing "You are so stupid," "You make me sick," or "I am sorry you were ever born" being repeated time and time again? That is exactly what it's like in the minds and homes of many young ladies you may come in contact with every day.

Low self-esteem in a young lady can be the cause of many unwise and unhealthy decisions. A young lady who doesn't value herself will often date young men who do not treat her with respect. She makes these choices unconsciously, because in her heart she may not feel she is worthy of love.

We attract others based on how we feel about ourselves. If the things I have shared with you so far suggest that you need to adjust your self-esteem, remember that it is possible for you to do so. Are you willing to work on adjusting your self-esteem? If so, continue to read.

First, you must know that there is nothing in your past that you can change, but you can change your present and your future. To overcome low self-esteem you must make a decision to forgive the primary people in your life for the things they did or failed to do, and for the things they said or failed to say. Forgiveness is a gift you give to yourself, as well as to others. It does not matter if they ask to be forgiven or if they ever admit their mistakes; you can still forgive them.

The Bible speaks a lot about forgiveness in many passages. Jesus gives us heartfelt examples of how it is possible to forgive the most unbelievable and worst wrongs. We see this in the words He uttered on the cross after He had been beaten, whipped, spat upon, and crucified by those He came to save. Jesus demonstrated the possibility of forgiveness in spite of what must have been unbearable pain. He said, *"Father, forgive them; for they know not what they do"* (Luke 23:34).

When the first Christian martyr, Stephen, was stoned, he cried out, *"Lord, lay not this sin to their charge"* (Acts 7:60). Through God's grace he was able to forgive his executors.

I do not know anyone who has had a perfect childhood. Often parents fall short in one way or the other because there are no perfect people. It is so important for you to believe you can move beyond the things you have experienced in your life thus far. If you are willing to make a decision to forgive those who have hurt you, you will have taken a giant step toward adjusting your self-esteem.

Secondly, you can work on the things about yourself that you can change, things that cause you to feel ashamed or inadequate. For example, if your reading is not at a comfortable level, and you become uneasy when asked to read aloud, set aside an hour a day to practice reading aloud. Practice can help to improve any area of deficiency. Also, ask a teacher to help you find a tutor. You will be surprised at how willing others are to help when you make an effort to help yourself.

Third, never say anything negative about yourself. Always speak positively, even if it means biting your tongue to stop yourself from speaking. Make positive affirmations to yourself throughout the day.

Fourth, ask the Lord to give you someone you can talk to about the areas that keep you from feeling good about yourself. Talking is excellent therapy. There is healing in saying out loud to another person what you feel inside. The person God will lead you to will know when to listen and when to respond. The Lord knows who is trustworthy. He may lead you to an older person with experience and wisdom. I believe that the Lord gives us everything we need to have a healthy life. His desire is that we help one another, and He is concerned about everything that concerns us. Our heavenly Father has promised to be our Counselor, and one of the ways He counsels us is through other people.

Finally, to overcome low self-esteem you will have to begin to see yourself as God sees you. Those negative tapes that have been playing over and over in your mind need to be erased and replaced.

Read the Bible. It is God's letter to you. In His word, He tells you how much you mean to Him.

In Zechariah 2:8 God tells us that whoever touches you, touches the apple of His eye.  Psalm 139:18 says that God's thoughts towards you are more than the sands of the

# Self-esteem Thermometer

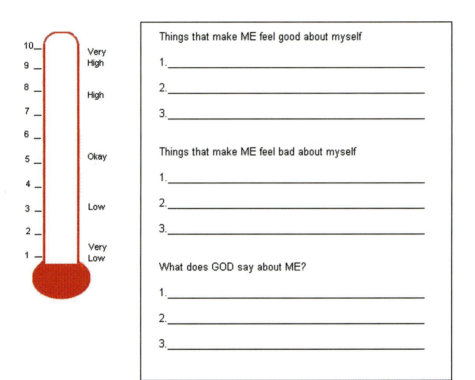

| | |
|---|---|
| 10 | Very High |
| 9 | |
| 8 | High |
| 7 | |
| 6 | |
| 5 | Okay |
| 4 | |
| 3 | Low |
| 2 | |
| 1 | Very Low |

Things that make ME feel good about myself

1._____

2._____

3._____

Things that make ME feel bad about myself

1._____

2._____

3._____

What does GOD say about ME?

1._____

2._____

3._____

sea.  In Revelation 1:6 we find that God calls us "kings and priests" (in our cases, queens and priestesses). The Bible has much more to say, but the only way you will know how God feels about you is to read His Word regularly and meditate upon its precepts faithfully.

Jesus thinks the world of you. He proved it by stretching out His arms and allowing nails to be driven through His hands on the cross. He allowed this because He had you on His mind. When the reality of this ultimate act of love truly penetrates your heart, you will realize that your worth is far above anything you could imagine.

In fact, it was God himself who determined your worth. The Bible is full of esteem-adjusting Scriptures like the ones you find in the two previous paragraphs. You should make a list of these verses and others like them and say them aloud to yourself every day. Remember, God has already given you everything you need to become the young lady He intended you to be – a young lady full of confidence – one who knows who she is in Christ.

Rebuilding a damaged self-image can be painful, and it definitely takes work, but the benefits are worth it. My hope is that you realize in your heart that you are special and worthy of all the good things this life has to offer,

regardless of what has happened in your past. I encourage not you to let your past determine your future!

# NOTES

# *Points to Remember*

**1.** Self-esteem is the value you place on yourself and the opinion you have of yourself.

**2.** Your sense of self-esteem is developed from the way you feel others see you.

**3.** If you have been given consistent affection and attention most of your life, chances are you have a healthy self-image. If the opposite is true, chances are your self-esteem needs to be adjusted.

**4.** Promiscuity is an attempt by some young ladies to reach out for love and acceptance.

**5.** When a young lady dresses in a way that draws attention to herself, she probably has low self-esteem and could be seeking the attention she has not received from her parents.

**6.** Here are five ways to overcome a low self-image:
    **A.** Forgive those who have mistreated or verbally abused you.
    **B.** Work on things you need to change.
    **C.** Never say negative things about yourself.
    **D.** Ask the Lord to show you someone to talk to about problem areas.
    **E.** See yourself the way God sees you by focusing on His Word.

*So God created man in his own image, in the image of God created he him; male and female created he them.*

*(Genesis 1: 27)*

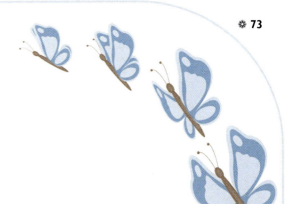

# NOTES

**Chapter 7**

*Your*

*Inner Beauty*

*D*id you know that facial beauty is greatly affected by inner beauty? However, inner beauty is much more difficult to cultivate, perhaps because it involves matters of the heart.

A heart full of bitterness, unforgiveness, envy, or jealousy certainly will overpower any positive physical attributes you may have. If you have a bad attitude, do not treat others with respect, have a haughty disposition, or are unkind in your treatment of others, you will not be admired or appreciated for your outer beauty.

Morgan, a senior high school student, told me about a disappointing experience she had with a friend:

# *Points to Remember*

**1.** Self-esteem is the value you place on yourself and the opinion you have of yourself.

**2.** Your sense of self-esteem is developed from the way you feel others see you.

**3.** If you have been given consistent affection and attention most of your life, chances are you have a healthy self-image. If the opposite is true, chances are your self-esteem needs to be adjusted.

**4.** Promiscuity is an attempt by some young ladies to reach out for love and acceptance.

**5.** When a young lady dresses in a way that draws attention to herself, she probably has low self-esteem and could be seeking the attention she has not received from her parents.

**6.** Here are five ways to overcome a low self-image:
  **A.** Forgive those who have mistreated or verbally abused you.
  **B.** Work on things you need to change.
  **C.** Never say negative things about yourself.
  **D.** Ask the Lord to show you someone to talk to about problem areas.
  **E.** See yourself the way God sees you by focusing on His Word.

*So God created man in his own image, in the image of God created he him; male and female created he them.*

*(Genesis 1: 27)*

# NOTES

*Morgan met April at summer school during her sophomore year. The first impression she had of April was a good one. Morgan liked the way April dressed and she admired her stylish haircut, which seemed to bring out the best in April's facial features. She looked like someone it would be nice to be friends with.*

*The two did become friends and before long were sharing lunch and spending time together after school. They had a lot in common: both liked to swim and both shared a lot of the same ideas about what they wanted to do with their lives after graduation. However, it did not take long for Morgan to realize that April, with her beautiful face, nice clothes, and stylish haircut, had a very negative way of expressing herself – she used a lot of profanity. At first, Morgan tried to overlook it, but it was difficult for her to do since it happened so frequently.*

*Morgan spoke to April several times about her use of profanity and how it made her feel uncomfortable. The two even came up with a plan to help April with her un-ladylike speech. Here is their plan: if April used a curse word in Morgan's presence she would have to give Morgan a quarter. They agreed that Morgan would drop the money in the offering basket at church each Sunday. The plan worked well for about a week before April was back to her old habit of attempting to draw attention to herself with her shocking language.*

*Morgan soon realized, that although she liked April, she did not want to be in her presence any longer if she couldn't express herself without using profanity as punctuation to her speech. It made her feel dirty to be around April. Her feelings about their relationship began to change, and she decided not to allow a more serious friendship to develop.*

Morgan realized that not only are persons known by the company they keep, but she also remembered the biblical teaching that evil communications corrupt good manners (1 Corinthians 15:33). This verse clearly means that we become like those we associate with.

Inner beauty cannot be achieved apart from a close relationship with Christ. Admitting where we are, and allowing the Lord to change us is the only way to be truly beau-

tiful. If you will read your Bible daily, spend time in prayer, and live according to God's Word, you will become truly beautiful, possessing the kind of beauty that does not fade with age – inner beauty that radiates from your face, your words, and your behavior.

### Stress Can Affect Inner Beauty

Do you ever feel as if you just can't take the pressures of life? Or are you sometimes so concerned about an upcoming exam that you are too uptight to study? Well, understand this: stress is a part of life, but you can learn to deal with any challenge that may come your way.

Incorporate these suggestions into your daily routine, and you will see that, with God's help you can overcome any situation or circumstance:

❑ Get into the habit of praying about everything. Your heavenly Father's ears are always open to your prayers.

❑ Pace yourself by not accepting too

many commitments. Prioritize, prioritize, prioritize.

❑ Get at least eight to ten hours of sleep each night. Your body needs time to rest, repair, and recuperate.

❑ Try a relaxing activity before going to bed to help slow down your mind and body. Try a warm bubble bath, a few stretches, or read a few chapters from a good book.

❑ Help your brain and body by eating healthy, nutritious foods. Limit empty calorie foods like candy, chips, and fast food.

❑ Don't be afraid to ask your family and friends for help. You were not created to go through life as "The Lone Ranger." Put your pride aside and ask for help.

❑ Keep your belongings as organized as possible in order to save time and keep yourself from any I-can't-find-it stress. Have a place for everything, and keep everything in its place.

❑ Remember to cast all your care on the Lord, because He cares for you (First Peter 5:7).

❑ Build yourself up by reading God's Word daily. When challenges come, the Word you have on the inside will rise up and go to work on your behalf.

# *Points to Remember*

**1.** Inner beauty cannot be achieved apart from a close relationship with God.

**2.** Inner beauty is much more difficult to cultivate than outer beauty because it involves matters of the heart.

**3.** Keeping company with the wrong people can affect the way others see you and the way you see yourself.

**4.** If you will read your Bible daily, spend time in prayer, and live according to God's Word, you will develop inner beauty.

**5.** Stress can cause acne and other physical problems.

**6.** A good, healthy diet and plenty of rest can help you with day-to-day stress.

*Search me, O God, and know my heart: try me, and know my thoughts:*

*And see if there be any wicked way in me, and lead me in the way everlasting.*                                                    *(Psalm 139:23-24)*

*NOTES*

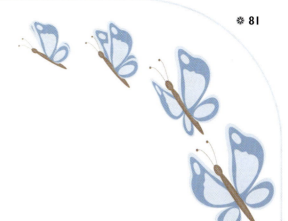

# Chapter 8

# *Skin Care*

While some teen-age skin may be normal to dry, most young ladies crashing through puberty tend to have oily skin. Because of the hormonal activity that goes on during adolescence, the skin may produce excessive amounts of oil, which can cause pimples and acne to emerge. This is why it is so important to begin a consistent skin-care routine.

When it comes to caring for your skin, make cleansing a ritual. Your skin needs the benefits of a facial cleanser that is specifically designed for your skin type.

## *Twelve Tips for Beautiful Skin*

❑   Use a sunscreen to guard against harsh rays when you're outdoors.

❑   Cleanse your skin thoroughly.

❑   Use only good cosmetics.

❑   Eat fresh fruits and vegetables frequently.

❑   Try to get eight to ten hours of sleep each night.

❑   Moisturize daily.

❑ Exercise regularly.

❑ Do not use regular body soap on your face.

❑ Use only clean cotton washcloths when washing your face.

❑ Use a deep-cleansing mask weekly.

❑ Apply beauty products in an upward-outward direction.

❑ Drink at least eight glasses of water a day.

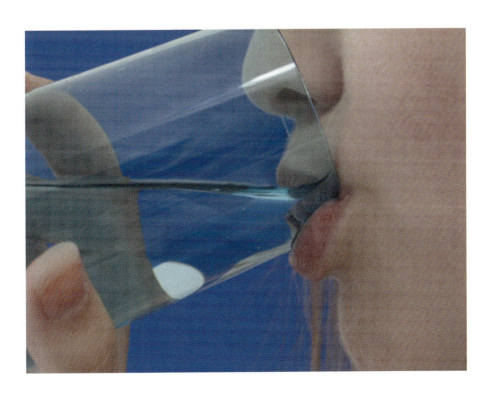

## The Four Skin Types

There are four basic skin types. It is important to know what type of skin you have, so you can use the right products to properly care for it.

**Normal** skin seldom has blemishes. It feels neither oily nor dry. It has a smooth, dewy look. If you have normal skin, to keep it looking youthful and healthy, don't spend long periods of time in the sun. To cleanse, use cleansing creams, a mild toner and a water-based moisturizer. Be sure to use good cosmetics at all times.

**Combination** skin is drier on the cheeks and around the hairline and oilier in the center of the face – the nose, the chin and the forehead. This area is called the "T" zone, because, from across the forehead down the bridge of the nose to the chin, is the shape of a T. After cleansing, use a lightweight moisturizer. Combination skin is the most common skin type.

**Oily** skin shines most of the time. If you have this type of skin, you can sometimes see large pores in your face, especially around your nose and cheeks, and you may have problems with blackheads or whiteheads. Oily skin should be cleaned at least three times a day. After cleaning, use a moisturizer containing alcohol so your skin will get the kind of deep cleansing treatment it needs.

**Dry** skin feels very tight and dry. There may be lines around the eyes and mouth. Dry skin usually has few blemishes and may look dull if not properly moisturized. If you have dry skin, avoid anything that will further dehydrate your complexion, such as alkaline soaps and excessive sunlight. Try to keep moisturizer on your face at all times.

## Caring for Your Face

There are three steps involved in caring for your face. They are cleansing, toning, and moisturizing.

Let's now look at each of these steps in detail. Cleansing will wash away the outer layer of dead skin cells, remove make-up and dirt and excess oils that can block pores, which

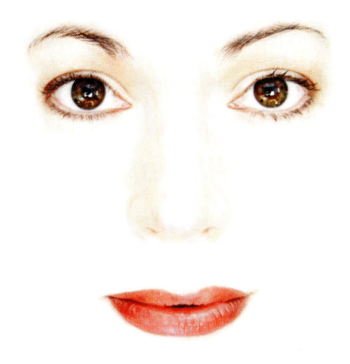

eventually develop into blemishes and promote a problem appearance.

Toning will stimulate and freshen your skin, remove left-over oils and cleansers, promote a
more youthful appearance and prepare your skin to receive the moisturizer, which is the last step.

Moisturizing will replenish moisture that has been lost due to cleansing and toning. It helps prevent dryness and gives your skin a soft, dewy glow. It also aids in providing longer wear for your makeup.

There are everyday facial cleansers that may be used on your face several times a day instead of soap, but it's perfectly all right to use soap if it is made especially for the face. There are also facial scrubs that are designed to stimulate circulation and remove dead cells.

Facial masks are deep cleansers that stimulate circulation, draw out impurities, and tone and firm your skin.

Moisturizers add water to skin cells, and they soften your face. Always use a moisturizer before applying your makeup.

What a difference good skin care will make in your appearance! Once you have mastered skin care, you are ready to consider makeup (only with the consent of your parents). Remember, good skin-care habits should be a part of your daily routine. When you begin to wear makeup, don't forget it is makeup, not makeover!

# *Points to Remember*

**1.** The four basic skin types are normal, dry, combination, and oily.

**2.** There are three steps in caring for your face – cleansing, toning, and moisturizing.

**3.** You need a cleanser specifically designed for your skin type.

**4.** Good skin-care habits should be a part of your daily routine.

**5.** Determining your skin type is critical to knowing how to care for your skin.

**6.** Be sure to use a sunscreen when going outside for long periods of time.

*And let the beauty of the Lord our God be upon us.*

*(Psalm 90:17)*

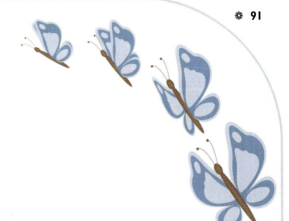

*NOTES*

# Chapter 9

# *Friendships*

*F*riends and friendship, sorta like kinship, without the blood bond... and although you feel like sisters... there was no wedding between Miss or Mister.

A godly bond is stronger than blood. A good friend is important to the mind, body, and soul, always there until you get old.

Exposing that friendly love, that warms the heart, being a good friend is a gift and an art.

To trust or be trusted with the most sacred secret, your friend prays to God that you can keep it.

A friend is there on troubled days, one who takes it to God's altar and prays. A friend's need is your sacrifice, so much so that you wouldn't think twice.

A godly friendship is strong, like a sturdy steel rod. Friendships are complimented, counseled, and created by God.

*– Written by J. Weise at age 16*

When I think of a friend, I think of someone who knows the worst about me and loves me anyway. I consider a friend someone I can share my feelings and thoughts with and know that I will not be judged.

True friends are a blessing from God. I believe God puts friends in our lives to help us, strengthen us, and give us the opportunity to strengthen others. Only God can knit two hearts together and enable them to feel so comfortable with one another that they can't – or won't – be separated.

The Book of Ruth is a wonderful expression of the life-changing, life-sustaining commitment of two women to one another. Both were widows. Ruth, Naomi's daughter-in-law, was still very young and beautiful after her husband died. Without a husband to tie her to her mother-in-law, Ruth could have returned to Moab, the land of her people, leaving Naomi to fend for herself during a time of famine.

Instead of abandoning Naomi, Ruth made this statement to her mother-in-law, which is recorded in Ruth 1:16:

*"… Intreat me not to leave thee, or to return from following
after thee: for whither thou goest, I will go; and where thou
lodgest, I will lodge: thy people shall be my people, and thy
God, my God."*

Take a few minutes before you lie down to sleep
this evening and read the entire Book of Ruth.  This
heartwarming account of one woman's devotion to
another is very moving. It is amazing to see how God
showed Naomi and Ruth how to support each other
when all seemed hopeless in both of their lives.
Because of this very special friendship between them
and their loyalty to each other, God's plan was
accomplished, and out of their family line the Savior
was born.

There's only one person who can fill the bill of a
perfect friend. His name is Jesus. He will never leave
you nor forsake you (Hebrews 13:5). He's a friend who
sticks closer than a brother (Proverbs 18:24). He will never
violate your confidence. He will never lie to you. He has
already given His life for you.

But there are some people on earth who may
qualify as the "perfect" friend, even though we know
that there are no perfect people. They qualify because
we love them so much we are willing to overlook their
human failings. We can never expect these "perfect"
friends to never make a mistake. If we do, sooner or later
we will be disappointed.

Forgiveness has to be a part of any friendship.  Our
heavenly Father demonstrates this every time we miss
the mark, because He forgives us immediately when we
ask Him to do so.  Since God is faithful to forgive, we
should be willing to do the same when our friends fail us

in some way.

What do you consider the most important ingredient in friendship and how would you rate yourself as a friend?

## *A Matter of Loyalty*

We need our friends desperately when we are going through difficult times, and those hard times have a way of revealing who our friends truly are. Loyalty says, "I will be there for you, no matter what."

I remember Kim, a young lady who was in my Sunday school class. She was about thirteen years old and very faithful in her attendance. One Sunday morning Kim brought her best friend, Anna, to class. Anna was also thirteen but she was very depressed. Kim knew the reason for Anna's depression, because Anna had confided in her. Kim not only invited Anna to Sunday school, but she also arranged for her mom to pick up Anna on that cold Sunday morning. The week before Anna had attempted suicide.

Anna wanted to take her own life because she had made a serious mistake. She allowed a young man in her neighborhood, someone she had secretly liked since she was in elementary school, to talk her into having sexual intercourse with him. The young man told Anna that he had admired her for a long time. He also told Anna, "If you let me, I will not tell anyone." Well, Anna let him, and he told everyone! She was deeply hurt and confused. Not only had Anna been betrayed by someone she trusted, but she had given him something very precious that can only be given once, her virginity. Like a pearl thrown to a pig, he had no appreciation of it.

Anna had to face all her peers at school, knowing they all knew. This devastated her. She took pills from her parents' medicine cabinet in an attempt to take her life. Anna said the hardest thing was the way her so-called friends treated her afterward – that is, everyone except Kim.

It broke Kim's heart to see Anna in such a miserable state. Kim did not stop being her friend after she learned of the mistake. She did not call Anna stupid, or a slut, like some of the other girls did. Kim even went the extra mile for her friend. She took her to a place where she believed her friend could receive help and encouraged her to talk to an adult about what she was going through.

Today, Anna is well past the crisis that almost took her life.

I recall sharing with Anna that God's forgiveness is hers for the asking, and that she also needed to forgive herself. At the time, she was still punishing herself for the mistake she made, and it was causing her great pain.

## *Permanent Solution, Temporary Problem*

I talked to Anna about suicide. I attempted to help her understand that suicide is a permanent solution to a temporary problem. I knew it was important for Anna to understand that the negative effects of this situation, what hurt her so deeply at that time would pass, and that she could get through it. I told Anna that suicide was too permanent a solution for any challenge in life. This was very necessary for Anna to understand, so, when she encountered other problems in life, she would never again consider suicide as a way out.

Anna did not try to take her life again. She made it through. Her friend Kim was right by her side, sharing her pain. Anna is very grateful to Kim, who showed her the true meaning of friendship, remaining loyal to a friend regardless of the circumstances.

Can the young lady you consider your best friend depend on you to be there to support her when she faces difficulties in life? Are you willing to share in your friend's sorrows as well as her joys? I hope your answer is yes, because only then will you be on the way to experiencing the true meaning of friendship.

## FOR GIRLS ONLY

*So you want to be popular and enjoy yourself while young*
*You want to be admired and have your praises sung.*
*And all of this is natural and ordained by God above.*
*But never try to prove yourself without a wedding ring.*
*And never deal in free love, for there is no such thing.*
*Free love is a sales pitch. It is a game you cannot win.*
*So do not risk your chances for a long and happy life.*
*A life of true fulfillment known only to a wife.*
*For regardless of society and the morals they disparage.*
*Nothing in the world can take the place of love and marriage.*

(Author unknown)

### *So You Wanna Be Popular*

I define popularity as being liked by many people or being well-known. How do you define popularity?

There are basically two ways to become popular, the world's way and God's way. If your desire is to be well-known, which way will you choose?

If you choose the world's way, it may be necessary to compromise your morals and your beliefs. Often young ladies go overboard in their attempts to be liked. Some join clubs, committees, choirs, and sororities in search of validation from their peers. Sometimes they follow the wrong crowd. That's why it's important to remember that not everyone is going to think you are the greatest, smartest, cutest, and the most athletic, regardless of how many extracurricular activities you involve yourself in. But why should you care?

Instead of attempting to find popularity the

world's way, why not do it God's way? Ask God to show you what specific activities you should become involved in. Remember, everything that concerns you concerns Him.

Proverbs 3:6 tells us: *"In all thy ways acknowledge him, and he shall direct thy paths."*

Popularity God's way is a much better choice.

Proverbs 16:7 explains: *"When a man's ways please the Lord, He maketh even his enemies to be at peace with him."*

## Why Friendships End

Two of the major reasons friendships between females are destroyed are envy and jealousy. I consider envy and jealousy twins, because where you find one, you will usually find the other.

Envy is the desire to possess something that someone else has. It means to be discontented because of another person's success, advantage, or position.

Jealousy involves anxiety, because you are suspicious of another person. Envy and jealousy are beauty-snatchers. They can make a pretty young lady appear very ugly. It is difficult to be around a person who has an envious or jealous spirit. These attributes can be seen in a look, a spoken word, or an attitude. It is impossible to hide these evil twins, regardless of how you might try.

You can guard your relationships from envy and jealousy by realizing that people are different in many ways.

Do not allow the strengths or advantages of others to cause you to become envious or jealous. You do have a choice. If these feelings surface, confess them to the Lord. Talk to your friend about what you are feeling. Satan uses envy and jealousy to end close friendships. Do not allow him to deceive you. Your God-given friendships are too valuable to allow yourself to give in to these beauty-snatchers.

# *Points to Remember*

**1.** Because of Ruth's loyalty to Naomi, she married into the line of ancestry that would eventually bring forth the Savior.

**2.** True friends are a blessing from the Lord.

**3.** Jesus is a friend who sticks closer than a brother.

**4.** Forgiveness has to be a part of friendship.

**5.** There are basically two ways to become popular, the world's way and God's way.

**6.** Envy and jealousy are the two main destroyers of female friendships.

*Iron sharpeneth iron; so a man sharpeneth the countenance of his friend.*                    *(Proverbs 27:17)*

*NOTES*

# Chapter 10

# *Christian Dating*

# The Compromise

*This young girl was born on a spring's dawn*
*She was soft and delicate as a little fawn*
*On a mission from God to sing and to dance*
*Her parents knew she had only one chance*

*She was raised in happiness*
*She knew the words of righteousness*
*She grew to be elegant, beautiful, and fair*
*With long, brown, soft, silky hair*

*She met a man on a summer's evening*
*The man turned out to be deceiving*
*He took her gift and tore it apart*
*For he also broke her heart*

*He took away her entire life*
*And left nothing but sorrow and strife*
*As for the man he was the devil in disguise*
*For he made her reach a compromise*

*Don't let the devil take authority over your life!*
*All that he will bring in will be sorrow and strife!*

*Everyone will see the tears in your eyes!*
*And all because of the Compromise!!*
*                   —by Amber Merchant at age 15*

You would probably agree that dating today means two people going out together without a chaperone. And you'd probably agree, like most teen ladies, that the right time to begin dating is as soon as you find that just-right guy who gets your heart flipping. Right?

But with dating comes heavy responsibility. It takes a strong young lady to spend time alone with a guy whose every glance makes you turn limp. That might be a little too much for most teens, so pay attention to the following suggestions:

You have to set firm limits concerning physical contact. You have to make some kind of decision about what, if any, touching is allowed, even down to holding hands. Some guys like to touch, and if you aren't real careful, they'll touch in ways that they shouldn't. You have to be firm from the start. It should never come to this, but if the young man's hands start to roam, that's the time to explain that this is something you won't tolerate.

You need to know what your standards are for selecting a guy to date. Do you like guys who are a little rough around the edges, or so shy you have to lead them? Do you prefer them so handsome that you can't stop admiring their looks, or the rugged-looking type? Do you prefer a Christian or a non-Christian? Your choices may have a lot to do with your motives for wanting to date.

Unless you know a young man pretty well, it's hard to predict how he'll act on a date. Just for safety's sake – his and your own – it's probably best to get to know him for a good while before going out alone. The first few dates should probably be at your home, where your mom and dad can observe him a little bit. You will get rid of a few pretenders that way.

There are other important questions you should ask yourself: Are you under control, or are you the one who's in the lead? If you're the aggressive type, you might want to dampen your speed a little. You don't want to lead the young man on or run him away. These are just a few of the questions you need to answer before you're prepared to spend time alone with any young man, including the guy of your dreams.

## How Ready Are You?

In earlier times – that's way back in the day – the purpose of one-on-one dating was to determine the compatibility of two people who had marriage on their minds. In our super-speedy, microwave world, we have dumped that original purpose. Many young ladies today start with the idea that the young man is cute. They may say, "I like him, and we want to date," before they even get to know the young man well.

Some teens date out of peer pressure. They don't want to be thought of as being dull or boring, so they pressure themselves to do things they aren't mentally ready to handle. You probably know some young ladies who have pressured their parents to allow them to date because "all their friends are dating." Dating because your friends are dating is usually not a good reason for you to date. If you're putting pressure on your parents, think about it for a moment. Do you really want them to do something against their better judgment? Are you

not mean you have to go all the way. She was very proud of the fact that Keith would stop when she asked him to. But Linda was mistaken for at least two reasons.

First, with such fondling she was bound to eventually get to a point where she did not want to tell him to stop. The flesh has its own will, and likes to be touched. Linda had already compromised herself too much by getting in the back seat with him. This was a definite green light to Keith to go further.

I told Linda that the more she gave in to her flesh, the more her flesh would want. This is why she allowed Keith to go as far as she had. Linda certainly did not imagine when they first kissed that she would ever allow him to touch her in the places she eventually allowed him to touch.

The second reason she was mistaken was because she cared deeply for Keith, and he knew it. Sooner or later he would begin to put more pressure on her to allow him to go further than she had before, and it would become more and more difficult for her to resist. His flesh was making demands on him, also.

I explained to Linda that she was putting Keith in a very unhealthy situation, and that she was tempting him to sin. Linda was arousing him sexually, and not being married to Keith, she was in no position to fulfill the desires she was awakening in him. It's a normal reaction for the body to progress from arousal to sexual intercourse. She was not treating Keith with respect, nor was she treating herself with respect.

I told Linda that she should not continue to put herself in the situation where she could compromise the high standard she had previously set, which was to remain a virgin until marriage. Linda was playing with fire, and she believed, rather foolishly, that she would not get burned.

*Rule Number One: No young man should be allowed to put his hands all over your body unless God has given you to each other in marriage.*

Needless to say, Linda did not take the advice she was given. She continued to allow herself to be in situations where she and Keith were alone together for long periods of time. They continued this physical relationship. Linda said several weeks later that she wished she had listened to the advice I had given her. Ultimately, she reached a point where she did not want to tell Keith to stop, and they went all the way. This all started from a single kiss three months earlier.

Regrettably, Linda's situation is quite common. Most teen ladies who become pregnant usually do so after dating a young man exclusively for several months. They may not have planned to become sexually involved, but they found it impossible to stick to the limits they had set prior to dating. This is why it is important not to pressure your parents to allow you to date, and not to sneak around to spend time with a young man.

Often, parents know your level of maturity better than you do. They have had the opportunity to watch you handle situations that require judgment and responsibility. There is so much more to life than dating at such a young age. Why make it such an issue?

*Rule Number Two: God's intent is that sex be an act performed by a male and female committed to loving each other for life. Sexual involvement, including kissing and petting, should not be a part of the dating experience.*

# *Points to Remember*

**1.** You should set firm limits concerning physical contact before dating.

**2.** It's best for Christians to date Christians because it's more likely that they will value the same things.

**3.** It is to your advantage to let God set the standard in choosing someone for you to date.

**4.** It's best to remain a virgin until marriage.

**5.** No young man should be allowed to put his hands all over your body unless God has given you to each other in marriage.

**6.** Sexual involvement, including kissing and petting, should not be a part of the dating experience.

*Be ye not unequally yoked together with unbelievers; for what fellowship hath righteousness with unrighteousness: and what communion hath light with darkness.*

*(2 Corinthians 6:14)*

*NOTES*

## Chapter 11

# *Your*

# *Wardrobe*

*S*tatistics show that teen girls spend about eighty-five billion dollars a year on fashion and beauty products. Fashion and beauty executives hire focus groups (groups of your peers – usually those with leadership qualities and the ability to influence), to wear their latest design concepts before the products are mass-produced. Members of the focus groups report back to the executives, and if their responses were favorable, ("Oooh, girl, where did you get that?"), then design items are churned out and shipped to a store in that area.

If the focus group's response is unfavorable, then it's back to the drawing board for the designers and executives. So, young lady, the low-hip jeans and the midriff-revealing tops that are so popular today, were more than likely the creation of a forty-five-year-old male fashion executive. Unknowingly, you and other young ladies are wearing clothing that older men want to see you wear.

This process of using focus groups is how fads are developed. The word fad could stand for (For a Day). To purchase a large quantity of fad items is a very expensive way to attempt to fit in with your peers and be accepted. Fads change so quickly, and most fads are not for every body type. When you choose to avoid spending your clothing allowance on the latest fad items and choose clothing that suits your body shape and is appropriately classic for your age, you will never have to be concerned about being embarrassed about the clothes you wear.

## *Code of Conduct*

There are some body parts that are considered private and definitely should not be revealed, regardless of the latest fad. In 1 Timothy 2:9, Paul urges that we adorn ourselves with modesty. I believe this urging by Paul is critical, because the way we choose to dress sends a message about our character, our self-esteem, our values, and our morals.

For the Christian females, there is a special code of conduct that should be followed in all that we do. We represent Christ, and there is no exception when it comes to our choice of dress. Your influence on others in your school, neighborhood, and family can very well begin with the way you dress. If you dress immodestly, others will not find you credible, even if you go to church every Sunday. The message you are sending by dressing immodestly is that Christ is not Lord of your life, at least in that area. His standard for your choice of dress is modesty.

What is the purpose of being refined, respectful, quiet, and gentle if your choice of clothing is based on fads and is crude and immodest? What messages are you sending when you wear such clothing? Should the fact that you belong to Christ make a difference in the clothes you wear? Most definitely.

Another point about immodest dress is that it attracts the wrong type of attention. The way females dress has a profound effect on males, old and young alike. Some females become aware of this fact at an early age and dress provocatively to get attention, perhaps because unconsciously they are looking for love and acceptance that may be lacking at home. Remember, this type of male attention does not come your way because you're such a nice girl. It's not based on the fact that you are trustworthy and a good student. This type of attention is purely physical, since men are stimulated by what they see. So any relationship developed from a situation such as that will not be lasting, nor will it be beneficial to you. By wearing provocative clothing, the message you are sending to young men is: This is what I have to offer you – my body.

## *The Modesty Test*

Try using these guidelines when you are shopping, to determine if the outfit you consider purchasing would pass the modesty test:

❐ Does this garment show my panty line?If so, it is probably too tight.

❐ Does my midriff show when I lift my arms? If so, try another shirt.

❐ Does this shirt pull across my bust line, making it difficult to move comfortably? If so, try a larger size.

❐ Does this garment show too much of my thighs or my panties when I sit? If so, try a different style, perhaps a fuller skirt, since skirts will always rise up when you sit down.

❐ Is this top so low that my cleavage shows? If so, you may want to layer your top by wearing a tee shirt under it, or by choosing another top that completely covers your chest.

## *Dress for the Occasion*

Deciding what to wear can be quite challenging. There are many things to take into consideration when choosing the right outfit: the time of day, the occasion, the type of event, and the location. Often, the invitation to a particular event will be the most helpful in making a choice regarding the appropriate style of clothing, because it usually contains all the information mentioned above. Be sure to ask for input from your parents when dressing for occa-

sions that you may not be familiar with – job interviews and formal and semi-formal events, for example.

## Your Individual Body Shape

Everyone can't wear everything, and they shouldn't try to do so. Only wear garments that fit your body well. Always try on clothing items before purchasing them, because clothes hanging on racks in stores can look deceptively right, but still be completely wrong for you. Wearing well-fitting clothing sends the message that you accept yourself just the way you are.

## Your Best Colors

Your choice of color is extremely important in looking your best. Although everyone can wear all colors, there are particular shades or hues that look best on you, based on your eye, hair, and skin color.

To determine what shades are best for you, hold the garment up to your face in good lighting. Does the garment make your eyes "pop" (appear bright)? Does it make

your skin look tired or pale, or bright and alive? Once you've tried a few garments based on this test, it will become easier for you to determine your very best colors. Every female should have a signature color. Your signature color is the one you look and feel your best in. To determine your signature color, pay attention to the comments you receive from others, and note how you feel when dressed in certain colors.

### Accessories

There is no area where modesty (restraint) should apply more than in the area of accessories. Although accessories can bring life to a plain, ordinary outfit, you always want to steer clear of that cluttered look. Avoid the temptation to keep adding more and more accessories. Rings on all four fingers, for example, is not as attractive as one ring tastefully placed on the pinky or forefinger. A belt, a scarf, and a necklace, for instance, can subtract from a

very nice outfit.    You don't want to dim your inner beauty by trying too hard with unnecessary outer adornments. Remember that there is elegance in restraint, and less really is better.

So whether you are shopping for that special-occasion outfit, or dressing for school or an evening out with your friends, remember that your choice of dress sends a message about you whether you are aware of it or not. Represent the Lord well in your dress, showing all who come in contact with you that you see yourself through His eyes, and not through the eyes of focus groups or fads, for, in His eyes, you are truly beautiful.

# *Points to Remember*

**1.** Your choice of dress sends out a message to others.

**2.** The time of day, the occasion, the type of event, and the location are the best clues to help you determine how to dress.

**3.** There is no area where modesty is more important than in the area of the accessories you choose.

**4.** Every female should know her signature color.

**5.** Always choose clothing that will complement your individual body shape.

**6.** Remember that in the area of accessories, less is better.

*In like manner also, that women adorn themselves in modest apparel, with shamefacedness and sobriety.*

*(1 Timothy 2:9)*

*NOTES*

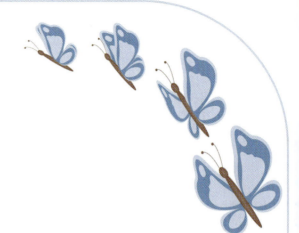

## Chapter 12

# *Your*

# *Queenly*

# *Posture*

*W*hat is posture?  Posture is the way you carry your body and the attitude you have while sitting, standing or walking.

There are many reasons to practice good posture. Have you ever seen a beauty pageant where the ladies came onstage slouched over? Not only are you more attractive when you walk upright, stand erect, and sit

with your legs together, but you have a better chance of developing strong back and neck muscles, as well.  You are at an age where your bones and muscles are still developing.  Sitting slumped over for long periods of time will almost guarantee that your spine will not develop properly.

The first impression others have of you comes from what they see with their physical eyes, and one of the first things people notice about a female is her posture.

If others form an opinion of you based on what they see, and since good posture is essential for proper muscle and back development, don't you agree that good posture is important for your overall development? Work on how you can develop good posture to make a favorable impression on others.

### What Does the Way You Walk Reveal About You?

Your walking posture tells those around you how you are feeling. If you are sad, tired or happy, it will show in your posture.

It is important for you to walk and stand with confidence. This means you should walk and stand with your head up as a demonstration of the God who lives within you. Taking small steps looks more feminine than taking long strides. Models are taught to practice walking with a book balanced on their heads. They learn by doing. It is impossible to balance a book on your head and walk with your head down.

How is your walking posture? Take about fifteen minutes a day and practice walking with your head up, shoulders back, and your back straight. Try to balance a book on your head as you take small steps.

### Sitting Pretty

Here are some posture pointers for you to incorporate into your life:

❑ Sit with your buttocks at the back of the sofa or chair. Your legs should be completely closed.

❑    To sit like a lady, allow the back of your knees to touch the front of the chair seat. Keep your back as straight as possible, but try not to look stiff.

❑    Never sit straddling a chair, even in a casual environment. This is very un-ladylike.

❑  While sitting, keep your legs together and your hands in your lap.

*Rule number three: It is always important to sit with your legs closed, whether you are wearing slacks or a dress.*

### Entering and Exiting an Automobile

Now for some tips about getting into and out of vehicles:

❏ The proper way to enter the front seat of an automobile is to put your buttocks in first, then use your arms and hands to balance yourself as you swing your legs in. To exit, reverse this procedure.

❏ When entering the back seat of a two-door automobile, it is almost impossible to enter in the same way as you would enter the front seat. Bend your upper body as little as possible as you put a foot and your head in first. If you are wearing a skirt or a dress, use your hand to make sure you are not exposing your rear end.

# *Points to Remember*

**1.** One of the first things people notice about you is your posture.

**2.** Your walking posture reveals how you're feeling.

**3.** It is un-ladylike to sit straddling a chair, even in a casual environment.

**4.** Ladies always sit with their legs closed, no matter what they are wearing.

**5.** Good posture helps your back and neck muscles develop properly.

**6.** Walking with a small stride instead of a long one always looks more feminine.

*I was also upright before him, and I kept myself from mine iniquity*                    *(Psalm 18:23).*

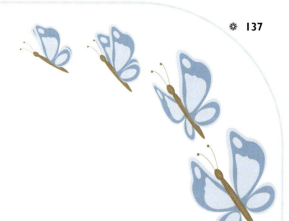

*NOTES*

## Chapter 13

# Telephone Etiquette
# and
# Common Courtesies

*W*hen calling the home of a close friend whose family you know well, have a relaxed, yet respectful tone of voice.

EXAMPLE: Hello, this is Tiffany. How are you? May I speak to Darlene, please?

When calling the home of someone you do not know well, or when calling for the first time, always introduce yourself before asking to speak to the person you are calling.

EXAMPLE: Hello, this is Tiffany Bridges. May I speak to Darlene, please?

### Receiving Telephone Calls

When answering the telephone at home, follow the guidelines your parents have set. If there are no guidelines, always answer with a cheery "hello." If the person the caller asks to speak to is not in, offer to take a message. Always repeat the message back to make sure you have taken it correctly. Make sure you put the message in a place where the person for whom it is intended will see it as soon as he or she arrives. It does no good to take a message for someone and not give it to them.

Treat any message you take for someone as though it is something very valuable, because it very well may be valuable to the person for whom it is intended. If you are home alone or without an adult, never tell the caller that your parents are not there. Instead, you may say they are not available at this time. Do not give out any information to anyone over the telephone if you do not know the caller. Many people in our society attempt to run scams by using

the telephone. If someone calls your home and asks questions about your family, chances are the information will not be used in your family's best interests. Be a wise young lady, and always be polite.

*Rule number four: Being polite does not mean doing whatever is asked of you by strangers.*

### Common Courtesy

Common courtesy simply means to make a habit of being polite. Doing so is a demonstration of respect for others. Using common courtesy should be such a part of your life that you exhibit courtesy without thinking about it. Make a habit of practicing common courtesy. Remember, the best place to practice it is at home, since we often take our family members for granted.

Being courteous to others is a way of showing respect for them. This includes our family. Otherwise, why be courteous to total strangers, and treat your family as if they are not worthy of respect? Although we feel better when others are courteous to us, we are not responsible for their behavior, only our own.

**Rule number five: Never allow another person's actions, however rude they may be, to determine your response.**

Some common courtesies to practice daily are:

❏   Always use the word `please` when you ask for something.

❏   Say, "Thank you," when you receive something.

❏   Say, "Excuse me," when you pass in front of someone.

❏   Say, "Hello," when you enter a room or see someone else enter.

❏   Say, "Hello," or "It is nice to meet you," when you are introduced to someone.

❏   Return what you borrow promptly (within twenty-four hours).

❏   Respect your friends' curfews.

❏   Respond quickly when you are called by a parent or a teacher.

❏ Await your turn in line patiently.

❏ Obey the rules of the group.

❏ Don't laugh at the mistakes and misfortunes of others.

❏ Don't take things that do not belong to you.

❏ Avoid loud and boisterous conversations.

❏ Call before you go to someone's home to visit.

❏ Don't give out other people's telephone numbers without their permission.

❏ Look a person in the eye when you converse with him or her.

❏ Answer with yes or no, instead of making grunts and sounds.

❏ Don't mark or write on walls and furniture.

❏ Return telephone calls promptly.

❏ Don't play your music so loud as to annoy others.

❐     Don't slam doors.

❐     Always offer your seat to an
       elderly person.

❐     Don't ever participate in gossip.

❐     In competition of any kind, always
       congratulate the winner.

❐     Never whisper to a person in
       front of others.

## *A Word About E-mail Etiquette*

E-mail etiquette, better known as NETIQUETTE, is simply common courtesy used in the online community.

When we communicate electronically, it is easy to forget that we are actually communicating with human beings. We cannot use our voice tones or facial expressions to help get our point across. The written word is all we have available to us. The written word is powerful, and it can be used to communicate the most serious or humorous feelings, if done so with sensitivity.

Follow these guidelines when using the Internet to communicate, and you will leave an impression of someone who is caring, sensitive, serious, and courteous.

❐     Do not type your e-mails in capital letters.
       This is regarded as SHOUTING.

❐     Do not write anything in an e-mail that
       you would not say to a person's face.

❐     Try to keep your communication short.
       The standard is no more than four lines.

A lot of people pay by the minute for their Internet service, and the longer your message, the more they pay.

❐ Remember that your e-mail communication may not be private. Once you've written it, you really do not have any idea who may have access to it.

❐ Be very selective in forwarding messages to your friends and relatives. Most people I have talked to, send the chain-type letters forwarded to them straight to the trash. (One person in particular sends me at least three or four forwards a week. Most of them are of no interest to me, so straight to the trash file they go.)

❐ There really is no need to send an e-mail with misspelled words. Be sure to check your spelling and grammar before hitting that send key.

❐ You should respond to an e-mail within twenty-four hours, the same as for telephone calls. If for some reason you could not respond within that time frame, be sure to address why you couldn't in your reply. No need to give out too many details, however.

I hope you enjoy using the Internet. It is fun, immediate, and a generally inexpensive way to communicate and explore. Don't forget that there are real people receiving your communications. Remember to be polite and appropriate in all your communications.

### *Etiquette for Introductions and Greetings*
Introductions should be pleasant, and greetings should always be warm and sincere. Eye contact and a firm hand-shake with a smile say to the person you are greeting that you are glad to meet him or her.

Introductions and greetings help people to feel com-fortable. There are certain guidelines to follow when intro-ducing one person to another. How should you respond when being introduced?

An older person is always introduced to an younger

person first. This is a way of showing respect for older people.

EXAMPLE: Sandy, this is my grandmother, Mrs. Ponce. Grandmother, this is my friend, Sandy Lewis.

Young men are introduced to young ladies before the young ladies are introduced.

EXAMPLE: James, I would like you to meet my friend Monique. Monique, this is James.

The proper response after being introduced to someone is "Hello," "How are you?" or, "It's nice to meet you."

When introducing an adult, always use Miss, Mrs., Ms., Mr., Dr., or whatever is appropriate for that particular person. The only time you may call an adult by his or her first name is when you have been given permission to do so by that adult and by your parents.

## The Handshake

A gentleman should wait for a lady to extend her hand before extending his. Women may shake hands with each other if they like.

Some are offended if you extend your left hand. In some cultures extending the right hand is considered to be a symbol of respect and honor.

Remember this:

***Etiquette is the formula of good manners, without which there would be no agreeable social relationships.***[1]

---

[1] **Encyclopedia Britannica, Vol. 8, University of Chicago, 1966.**

# *Points to Remember*

**1.** Never give out any information over the phone to a caller you do not know.

**2.** Introductions should be pleasant and greetings should always be warm and sincere.

**3.** The only time you may call an adult by his or her first name is after you've been given permission to do so by the adult and by your parents.

**4.** You practice common courtesy when you make a habit of being polite.

**5.** Never allow another person's actions, however rude, to determine your response.

**6.** A warm smile and a firm handshake say to the person you are meeting that you are glad to meet them.

*Finally, be ye all of one mind, having compassion one of another, love as brethren, be pitiful, be courteous.*

*(1 Peter 3:8)*

*NOTES*

**Chapter 14**

# Table/Restaurant Etiquette

*T*he practice of using good table manners helps to make the eating experience pleasant for all who are present. It is a way of showing respect for yourself as well as others.

Good table manners essentially come from doing what is most logical in the present situation. The main thing to remember is to eat without being self-conscious. To have good table manners requires practice, and the best place to practice is at home.

## TABLE ETIQUETTE

### *Your Table Posture*

The following recommendations will help you gain respect from others:

❐ Your hands should be in your lap when you are not eating. You should sit straight in your chair at the dinner table.

❐ You may rest your elbows on the table between courses, but never while eating.

❐ Keep your hands close to your body, so you do not interfere with those who are sitting beside you.

❐ Do not talk with your mouth full. This is unpleasant for others at the table who may not be able to understand what you are saying. Also, when you talk with food in your mouth, you take the chance of spraying someone else's plate or person with your half-chewed food, or getting the food lodged in your windpipe.

❐ Once you have put food on your fork or spoon, eat it right away.

❐ Put your napkin in your lap as soon as you are seated, but there are exceptions to this rule. At a formal dinner, the waiter may put it in your lap for you.

❐ Never use your personal utensils in the common serving dish.

❐ Be sure to chew your food with your mouth closed.

❐ Used knives and forks are never placed directly on the table.

❐ If you spill something, apologize and offer to clean it up. Accidents do happen, and there is no reason to feel embarrassed if one happens to you. At a restaurant, in order to avoid a safety hazard, alert the waiter or waitress if you have spilled something on the floor.

❐ Always wait for the hostess to tell you where to sit unless there are place cards, in which case you may take your seat once dinner has been announced.

## *The Place Setting*

A place setting is the arrangement of individual dishes, glasses, and flatware for each diner. All tables are set alike, which means they are set to accommodate right-handed people.

All place settings should be an equal distance from one another, and enough space should be allowed between them to make eating a comfortable experience for all those at the table.

*INFORMAL PLACE SETTING*

*FORMAL PLACE SETTING*

### Utensils

Forks and knives are arranged in the order of their use. If the setting is confusing to you, watch the host or hostess to see which is used first. If you use mealtime at home to practice, you will not risk feeling uncomfortable in a public setting.

At a formal setting, the butter knife should already be on the bread plate when you arrive at your table. Sometimes a fork or spoon is placed above the dinner plate in a horizontal position for your dessert.

### Restaurant Etiquette

There are basically five different types of restaurants. Each has a specific way of operating and each has an accepted dress code. Let's look at them in detail:

*1)Fast-food restaurants* may well be your favorite kind of eating establishment. Such places as McDonalds, Taco Bell, Wendys, Jack in the Box, and Burger King are in the fast-food category. The appropriate dress for such an eatery is from casual to extreme casual. In fast-food restaurants, orders are placed from an order line, or at a drive-through window. If you choose to eat inside, be sure to decide what you want to order before you get to the front of the line. As you probably have experienced, it can be
annoying to stand behind someone who cannot make up his or her mind as to what they want to eat.

People often go to fast-food restaurants because they are in a hurry and want their food quickly, and because meals are usually not very expensive as compared to other restaurants. Drivers often pull into fast-food restaurants, order a quick meal, and virtually inhale it as they continue on their way.

In fast-food restaurants, you sit wherever you like. It is your responsibility to remove your tray, food wrappers, napkins, and cups when finished, leaving your table free and somewhat clean for the next diner. Tipping is not necessary in a fast-food restaurant, but don't forget to use the words please and thank you when speaking to the person who takes your order and presents your food to you.

*2) The cafeteria, or buffet-style restaurant,* is also very popular with teen-agers and gives diners plenty of choices. Hometown Buffet and Souplantation are two well-known buffet-style restaurant chains in California. Usually, in such places, your utensils will be wrapped in a napkin, either cloth or paper, and are stacked near clean plates for convenience. In these restaurants, diners usually seat themselves. Most buffet-style restaurants have staff people who refill your drinks and remove your tray and dishes at the end of your meal. When you are finished, you should leave a tip for the person who clears your table. A maximum of $2.00 per diner is appropriate, instead of the customary fifteen or eighteen percent. The appropriate dress for this type of restaurant is casual.

*3) More formal restaurants* usually require reservations. Upscale dress is often expected in these establishments. This means no jeans, caps, or flip-flops, please! Some formal restaurants may even require men to wear ties. If you arrive at a formal restaurant improperly dressed, you may still be allowed to dine, but you may not enjoy the experience as much as you might have if you were dressed properly for the occasion. It is a good idea when calling to make your reservation at a formal restaurant to also ask about their dress code.

In some formal restaurants, the prices are not listed on the menu, and in others there may be no menu at all. Imagine that! The waiter or waitress will tell you what is being served, so you will definitely have to use your listening skills in this type of restaurant.

In most formal restaurants a gratuity (automatic tip) of fifteen to eighteen percent or more may be added to the check before it arrives at your table. If you are with a large party, you should expect that there will be a fifteen-to-eighteen percent gratuity added.

*4) Family-style restaurants* like Denny's, Coco's, Chili's and the International House of Pancakes, are casual. Family-

style restaurants usually cater to the entire family, including special food selections for little ones.

Reservations are usually not required, but you may have a wait when you arrive. Your utensils are often wrapped in a napkin, just as they are at buffet-style restaurants, but are already placed at the table. Some family-style restaurants have specialties like barbecue ribs, Chinese, Italian, Mexican, or other kinds of foods. Tipping is expected. The customary fifteen percent is usually appropriate.

*5) Quaint, specialty restaurants* are among my favorite places to eat. One in the city of Pasadena, California, where I live, is called the Tea Rose Garden. I often go there with young ladies to celebrate their completion of the personal development program I teach, the program that inspired this book.

The atmosphere at the Tea Rose Garden is titillating to the senses. Fresh flowers adorn each table and there are gorgeous teapots and other accessories displayed for purchase. There is also a beautiful fountain with fresh running water in the middle of the room. The food is delicious. True authentic English high tea delicacies are offered, such as scones and finger sandwiches, as well as fresh fruit and a variety of hot or iced teas and fresh salads. This type of specialty restaurant is very popular for small birthday parties and other "girly" celebrations. Hungry yet?

## HOW TO SIGNAL THE SERVER WHEN RESTING
### REST POSITION
(I Would Like More Time; Don't Touch My Plate!)

## HOW TO SIGNAL THE SERVER WHEN FINISHED

### FINISHED POSITION
(Please Take My Plate)

## Bon appetit!

There are ways to signal a waiter or waitress when you are finished eating. A waiter or waitress who know their craft do not have to continue to ask you if you are finished with your meal. They can read the signs you leave. Above are ways to indicate to your server if it's okay to take your plate, or if you are still enjoying your meal.

# *Points to Remember*

**1.** Practicing good table manners is a way of showing respect.

**2.** A place setting is the arrangement of individual dishes, glasses, and flatware for each diner.

**3.** Unless there are place cards, always wait for the hostess to tell you where to sit.

**4.** A tip of at least fifteen percent is customary in family-style and formal restaurants.

**5.** Reservations are usually required at formal restaurants.

**6.** Never use your personal utensils in a common serving dish.

**Whether therefore you eat, or drink, or whatever ye do, do all to the glory of God.**

*(1 Corinthians 10:31)*

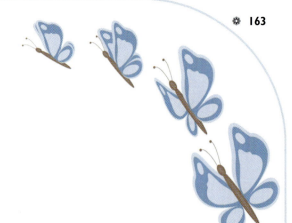

*NOTES*

## Chapter 15

# *Discovering*
# *Your Gifts*
# *&*
# *Talents*
### *(Your Life's Purpose)*

*E*sther of the Bible was a charming young lady, and she was very wise beyond her years. She had been raised as an orphan, and God used her greatly to accomplish His purpose to save her entire nation.

Though God had a purpose for her life, Esther still had to make difficult choices. Can you imagine an orphan girl who had lived a very conservative and quiet life suddenly being chosen to live in the king's palace

along with several other women? At each critical stage in her life Esther was wise enough to seek an answer from God, whom she was raised to love and serve.

Esther never forgot that she was, like you, a very special child of the Most High God. When her cousin, Mordecai, helped her to understand her purpose for

being in the king's palace, she trusted him and did not rebel against that purpose, though it could have cost her life. Her obedience allowed her to save her people, the Jews, from destruction.

Are you sometimes rebellious when your parent or guardian suggests that you conduct yourself in a particular way? Do you change your attitude by being argumentative or sullen? If so, learn to follow Esther's example.

*Rule number six: Favor in the sight of God can put you in the king's palace, and give you enough influence to change a nation.*

What thing has God purposed to accomplish in your life? What desire has He placed in your heart? What gifts and talents has He given to you that He wants you to perfect?

You must realize that nothing about your life is a mistake – not the family you were born into, the color of your skin, the shape of your nose, the shape of your eyes, and even the texture of you hair. Everything about you fits into God's purpose for your life, just as it did with Esther. She did not have a mother or father to help teach and train her, but she was raised well by her cousin. She may have had many insecurities, and feelings of rejection may have been overwhelming for her at times, but Esther became a perfect example of God's love and grace. The things that are most challenging in our lives are often the very things God uses to shape us and mold us into His image.

God's desire is for you to discover what He wants to accomplish in the earth through you. You are His precious gift to the world. The question is what are you going to do with what you have been given? You, too, have choices.

## *Choosing Your Life's Work*

If you marry, you may decide never to work outside the home. You may shift from one career to another, as you mature and your interests change or as you discover new gifts and talents. Whatever you choose, I can certainly say from experience that there is no greater joy than choosing work that you enjoy.

You may have gifts and talents that could be a source of great wealth to you. A gift or talent is a natural, God-given ability. Your gifts may be things you do well without much effort, or something you've learned easily and perfected in an unusually short amount of time.

Perhaps you enjoy working with children or organizing projects. Maybe you have the ability to listen to others and give wise counsel. Our gifts and talents are usually things that are natural for us.

Choosing to work in the area of your gifts and talents can bring contentment that you may not find in other areas of work. Do not be afraid to explore your gifts, and work on perfecting them. Learn all you can about them. By all means, when considering a career, don't overlook your natural gifts and talents as the most obvious directions for your career.

As you begin to consider your career path, always remember that the source of your income is never your job. Jobs are only a vehicle for God's provision. God is always your source. If your job was your source and you lost it, you could become emotionally devastated and extremely depressed.

Your source is and will always be your heavenly Father. He alone gives you the power to obtain wealth (Deuteronomy 8:18). Your hope and trust should be in Him, knowing that He is in control of every area of your life. As you submit to Him, there is no doubt that He will keep His Word and meet every one of your needs.

### *Preparing the Job Application*

In the process of looking for a job, the application you submit is your ticket to an interview. A good application will open the door, while a bad application may keep you unemployed. Obtain the following documents, and use the following tips to help you complete the job application in a way that will enable you to get your foot in the door:

❑ A birth certificate

❑ A Social Security card

❑ A drivers license

❏ A work permit (if required)

❏ At least three references (persons other than your relatives that you have known for at least one year, including their addresses, telephone numbers, and occupations). Be sure to get permission ahead of time from these references.

*Rule number seven: It is bad manners to list people as references without first getting their permission to do so.*

You will need information about any past work experiences: employers names, addresses, and phone numbers; dates of your last employment, salary, and reasons for leaving. You may be asked the names of your immediate supervisors on previous jobs. If you are applying for your first job, don't be concerned about not having information for this part of the application. Be sure to write "N/A," or "not applicable" in the space provided for past employment.

### Follow Instructions

If the instructions are in writing, read them thoroughly. If they are given orally, listen carefully, take notes, and ask questions. While filling out the application, be careful not to leave any blank spaces unless you are told to do so. If you leave something blank, the person who reads the application will not know if you omitted the answer by mistake, or if you intentionally chose not to give the information requested. If a question does not apply to you, simply write "N/A" in the answer space. If for some reason you do not know the answer, write in the word unknown, and get the missing information as soon as you can.

### Be Neat

If possible, leave no fingerprints or smudges on the application. If you take the application home, type it or have it typed, if possible. If you complete it in the office, print neatly. Whatever you do, be sure the person who reads it will not have to ask, "What does this say?"

Keep in mind that during the interview process you are dealing with professionals. They take their work seriously and expect you to do the same. When you are asked a question, tell the truth, and pay attention to details.

If you are asked to return your application by a specific day, get it back the day before it is due. That shows your prospective employer that you care about the job. If you are not told when to return it, take the application back the next working day. Your promptness will demonstrate your interest and efficiency.

### *The Interview*

Be sure to arrive at the interview at least fifteen minutes ahead of time. This means you must consider travel time, traffic, and parking if you want to get there early. Some job-hunters will scout out the potential employment site first by making a "dry run" before the day of the interview to find the location and test traffic conditions. If you arrive late, you make a bad first impression. Not only does lateness signal that you are not prompt, but it may make you a nervous wreck from worrying about getting off on the wrong foot. If the company facility is a big one, allow yourself enough time to find the office where the interview is being conducted.

Whatever the job or position, there is a standard you should follow when deciding what to wear to an interview. Always wear a dress or skirt. Wear plain colors as opposed to prints. Decide what to wear several days in advance. In this way you won't find yourself fretting on the day of the interview over a missing button or a run in your panty hose.

The way you enter the interviewer's office can make or break your meeting with him or her. Walk with your head up, your back straight, and have a pleasant attitude. The first impression you make is crucial. Show that you are someone who is pleasant and interesting.  You will never get another chance to make a first impression.

Don't allow yourself to relax too much if you think you are making a good impression.  It is never a good idea to get too comfortable in your chair or to act too familiar during the interview.  Keep good posture throughout the process.  As the interviewer discusses the job, pay attention to his or her attitude, as well as what he or she is saying.  You should read the interviewer just as the interviewer is reading you.  As you listen, ask yourself: "Is this a company I want to work for?  Will the salary offered meet my needs? Do the hours for this position fit into my schedule? Is this job in line with my gifts and talents?  Does this job hold the possibility for advancement?  Is this job challenging enough to hold my interest? Is this where God wants me at this time?"

## *Don't Be Anxious*

Your role throughout the interview is to keep your poise, and to respond clearly to any questions that may be asked.  No matter how long the interview continues, you may not know at its conclusion whether or not you have been hired.  In most cases you will have a lot of competition for the job.  The interviewer may see other prospects before or after you.  You may be called back for a second or third interview.  Remember, keep your poise through it all.

While there is no benefit in concentrating on the negative, one can benefit from knowing the six reasons why most people fail their interviews.  Listed below are the "big bad six":

❑ Poor appearance

❑ Inability to express views clearly

❑ Failure to project yourself confidently

❑ Failure to project enthusiasm

❑ Being overcritical of former employers

❑ Evidence of job-jumping

At a job interview you are selling yourself. Only when you have succeeded in selling yourself can you go on to sell your skills and potential. This is a basic reality of any job interview.

## *Discovering Your Gifts and Talents*

To help you discover your gifts and talents, please place a check mark by the statements that describe you best.

❑  I enjoy doing things for other people.

❑  I have a lot of ideas and a good

imagination.

❏ I love to encourage others.

❏ I am a good organizer; I love to make things run smoothly.

❏ I am able to save and manage money well; I also like to give money or gifts to people or causes that are in need.

❏ People tell me I'm easy to talk to.

❏ It seems as though I can stay calm in the middle of a crisis, even though those around me are in a panic.

❏ People often tell me that I have a nice smile.

❏ People tell me they feel better after sharing their problems with me.

❏ I love to make speeches and address large groups of people.

❏ I catch on easily to new songs and musical instruments.

❏ I enjoy cooking, trying new recipes and entertaining.

❏ I enjoy entertaining guests in my home and making them feel comfortable.

❏  I enjoy writing in my journal and/or composing lyrics for songs.

❏ It bothers me when I see misspelled words or words used incorrectly.

❏  I love being around children. It bothers me to see them unhappy.

❏ Somehow I always end up being the leader in a group.

❏ People always seem to come to me for answers.

# *Points to Remember*

**1.** Favor in the sight of God can put you in the king's palace.

**2.** Everything about you fits into God's purpose for your life, just as it did with Esther.

**3.** Whatever the job or position you are applying for, there is a standard you should follow when deciding what to wear to an interview. Always wear a dress or skirt and wear plain colors as opposed to prints.

**4.** On a job interview, the first impression you make is crucial. Show that you are someone who is both pleasant and interesting.

**5.** At a job interview you are selling yourself. Be enthusiastic and project confidence.

**6.** Give yourself plenty of time to get to the interview.

*A man's gift maketh room for him, and bringeth him before great men.*

*(Proverbs 18:16)*

*On the following page is a copy of a standard employment application. When filling out an actual application, be sure to follow all the instructions you are given. If possible, have a parent review your application after completion.*

## EMPLOYMENT APPLICATION

**PRINT OR TYPE–**

| APPLICANT'S NAME *(Last)* | | *(First)* | | *(M.I.)* | SOCIAL SECURITY NUMBER |
|---|---|---|---|---|---|
| MAILING ADDRESS *(Number)* | *(Street)* | E-MAIL ADDRESS | | | WORK TELEPHONE NUMBER |
| *(City)* | | *(County)* | *(State)* | *(Zip Code)* | HOME TELEPHONE NUMBER |

EXAMINATION(S) OR JOB TITLE(S) FOR WHICH YOU ARE APPLYING

FOR SPOT EXAMINATIONS, ENTER THE LOCATION WHERE YOU WISH TO WORK _____

**ANSWER THE FOLLOWING QUESTIONS:**

Enter the county in which you would like to take the
examination if different from the county of your residence: _____

Do you need reasonable accommodation to take an interview or written test? ............... ☐ YES ☐ NO

Do your religious beliefs prevent you from taking an examination on Saturday? ............... ☐ YES ☐ NO

Are you now employed      (If "YES", fill in the information below.) ............... ☐ YES ☐ NO
Department:——————————————————— Subdivision: ———————

Have you ever been dismissed or terminated from any position for performance or other disciplinary reasons? (Applicants ☐ YES ☐ NO
whose dismissals or terminations were overturned, withdrawn [unilaterally or as part of a settlement] or revoked need not
answer "Yes".)
If "Yes, refer to the Instructions for further information.

In addition to English, list any other languages you:
    a.    possess verbal fluency in _____
    b.    possess written fluency in _____
I certify I can type at a speed of _____ words per minute. (For typing applicants only.)

Do you meet the minimum and/or maximum age requirements? ............... ☐ YES ☐ NO

Do you possess a valid Driver License?      (If "YES", fill in the information below.) ............... ☐ YES ☐ NO
License# _____ Class: _____ Restrictions: _____
Have you ever been convicted by any court of a misdemeanor crime of domestic violence? ............... ☐ YES ☐ NO
Have you ever been convicted by any court of a felony? ............... ☐ YES ☐ NO

EXPLANATIONS

**CERTIFICATION–IMPORTANT–PLEASE READ BEFORE SIGNING–If not signed, this application may be rejected.**

*I certify under penalty of perjury that the information I have entered on this application is true and complete to the best of my knowledge. I further
understand that any false, incomplete, or incorrect statements may result in my disqualification from the examination process or dismissal from employment*

| APPLICANT'S SIGNATURE | DATE SIGNED |
|---|---|
| ✍ | |

*NOTES*

*Lord*
*let your reflection*
*in me,*
*be a light for all the*
*world to see.*

# Eating Disorder Treatment Centers

*T*he following list of inpatient/residential facilities was taken from the National Eating Disorders Association website. There are many other centers not named here. Your personal physician may be able to direct you to a more appropriate one near you.

| Organization Name | City | State | Telephone |
|---|---|---|---|
| Remuda Ranch Programs for Anorexia and Bulimia | Wickenburg | AZ | 800-445-1900 |
| Laureate Psychiatric Hospital and Clinic | Tulsa | OK | 918-491-3700 |
| Laurel Hill Inn | Medford | MA | 781-396-1116 |
| University Medical Center at Princeton | Princeton | NJ | 877-932-8935 |
| Eating Disorders Association of New Jersey | Metuchen | NJ | 732-549-6886 |
| Avalon Centers, Inc. | Williamsville | NY | 716-839-0999 |
| University of Rochester | Rochester | NY | 585-275-7844 |
| The Penn State Eating Disorders Program The Milton S. Hershey Medical Center | Hershey | PA | 717-531-7235 |
| The Renfrew Center | Ridgewood | NJ | 1-800-Renfrew |
| The Renfrew Center | New York | NY | 1-800-Renfrew |
| The Renfrew Center | Coconut Creek | FL | 1-800-Renfrew |
| The Renfrew Center | Philadelphia | PA | 1-800-Renfrew |
| The Renfrew Center | Wilton | CT | 1-800-Renfrew |
| The Bellott Clinic, Inc. | Woodstock | GA | 404-247-3425 |
| Wekiva Springs Wellness Center for Women | Jacksonville | FL | 904-256-3533 |
| Canopy Cove Eating Disorder Center | Tallahasee | FL | 850-893-8800 |
| CARE Inc. & PTA | North Palm Beach | FL | 561-494-0866 |
| Turning Point of Tampa | Tampa | FL | 813-882-3003 |

| | | | |
|---|---|---|---|
| Fairwinds Treatment Center for Anorexia and Bulimia | Clearwater | FL | 800-226-0301 |
| Scales Nutrition and Wellness Center | Nashville | TN | 615-284-4432 |
| Vanderbilt University Medical Center | Nashville | TN | 615-936-0252 |
| Rogers Memorial Hospital | Oconomowoc | WI | 800-767-4411 |
| Waukesha Memorial Hospital | Waukesha | WI | 262-928-4036 |
| Methodist Hospital Eating Disorders Institute | St. Louis Park | MN | 800-862-7412 |
| Eating Disorder Institute | Fargo | ND | 800-437-4010 |
| Rimrock Foundation | Billings | MT | 800-227-3953 |
| Alexian Brothers Behavioral Health Hospital | Hoffman Estates | IL | 847-822-1600 |
| Illinois Institute for Addiction Recovery | Peoria | IL | 800-522-3784 |
| St. Louis Behavioral Medicine Institute | St. Louis | MO | 636-532-9188 |
| Castlewood Treatment Center | Ballwin | MO | 636-386-6611 |
| McCallum Place on the Park | Clayton | MO | 800-828-8158 |
| Children's Hospital Eating Disorders Program | Omaha | NE | 888-216-1860 |
| River Oaks Hospital | New Orleans | LA | 800-366-1740 |
| Laureate Psychiatric Clinic & Hospital | Tulsa | OK | 800-322-5173 |
| Children's Medical Center | Dallas | TX | 214-456-8980 |
| The Menninger Clinic | Houston | TX | 800-351-9058 |
| Cadwalder Behavioral Clinics | Tomball | TX | 866-351-6644 |
| Shades of Hope Treatment Center | Buffalo Gap | TX | 915-572-3843 |
| Center For Change | Orem | UT | 888-224-8250 |
| New Life Centers | Salt Lake City | UT | 888-281-3353 |
| Avalon Hills Residential Eating Disorders Program | Petersboro | UT | 800-330-0940 |
| Mirasol, Inc. | Tucson | AZ | 888-520-1700 |
| Pia's Place | Prescott | AZ | 928-445-5081 |
| A Sober Way Home, Inc. | Prescott | AZ | 928-443-1764 |
| Center for Hope of the Sierras | Reno | NV | 775-828-4949 |
| Monte Nido Treatment Center | Malibu | CA | 310-457-9958 |

| | | | |
|---|---|---|---|
| Del Amo Hospital | Torrance | CA | 310-530-1151 |
| Rader Programs | Oxnard | CA | 800-841-1515 |
| Rader Programs | Tulsa | OK | 800-841-1515 |
| Puente De Vida | San Diego | CA | 858-581-1239 |
| South Coast Medical Center | Laguna Beach | CA | 949-499-7504 |
| Kartini Clinic | Portland | OR | 503-249-8851 |
| The Center for Counseling & Health Resources, Inc | Edmonds | WA | 425-771-5166 |
| Children's Hospital and Regional Medical Center | Seattle | WA | 206-987-3886 |
| Bellwood Health Services Inc | Toronto | ON | 800-387-6198 |
| Westwind Eating Disorder Recovery Centre | Brandon | MB | 888-353-3372 |

# FRUITION MINISTRIES

## *Balance*

We'll help your daughter get and keep hers.
As young ladies struggle with low self-esteem, identity crises, and temptations to settle for less, balancing God's design for their lives with worldly attractions can be a difficult act – but not an impossible one.

Fruition, our personal development program designed from the biblical prospective, offers courses and workshops that introduce young ladies, ages twelve to eighteen, to the gifts God has given them.

Our instructors are highly trained, skilled professionals with a burden to see young ladies become all they can be. Visit **www.fruitionministries.com**, or contact Johnnie Payne directly at **johnnie@fruitionministries.com**, and schedule a workshop or seminar for your group of young ladies. Help them balance God's design for their lives in an ungodly world.

# TESTIMONIES FROM TWO WHO CAME INTO FRUITION

### The Chocolate Blossom

At the age of twelve, my mother forced me to attend a Sunday school class that was being taught at our local church for young girls to learn etiquette, self-esteem, and Christian demeanor. Of course, I unwillingly attended with my friends. The class turned out to be fun, exciting, and worth the experience. However, in being a child and dealing with other children, problems still arose and my self-esteem was lost. I am a chocolate girl and was criticized for it, daily.

The Fruition classes taught me self-esteem, but the daily truth of criticism overpowered what I was taught. As a child, what I was taught contrasted greatly with my day-to-day adversities. Because of this, my demeanor was altered and I felt I had to "find my place in the world" to acquire friends. I wanted everyone to like me, but didn't know how to make it happen. I became a loud, obnoxious, Miss-Talk-A-Lot person that everyone knew but didn't really like.

I craved attention and this was the only way I saw to get it. I was popular because I was loud. I was disliked because I was loud and dark-skinned. I was talked about because I was loud and dark-skinned. However, through all this, I managed to find some solace through true friends who attended the same Fruition class. They knew I wasn't liked very much but, as friends do, they stood behind me, shielding me from the negative opinions of others.

Years later, I realized what the secret was. If I had just been myself, I now believe all would have worked out differently and better. I still would have incurred the criticism for my darker skin, but I would have been able to handle it better without damaging and scarring my self-esteem. If I had truly heeded the biblical verse embedded within our Fruition teachings – "You are beautiful and wonderfully made by God" – I would have been a completely different person. Period.

Completely reluctant at first, I was fortunate enough to return to my roots and assist with the Fruition class I attended years ago. I didn't think I was "lady" enough to teach, assist, or be an example of *A Lady by Choice* to the next generation of teen-agers. I wasn't for the first group, so I thought. However, I realized it wasn't about what I was doing for them. It was about what God was doing for me. In listening to the same lessons, I was taught over ten years ago, I was able to revisit some of the things I had lost, forgotten or missed. And, as I later found out, the teen-agers learned a lot from me, the assistant. Due to common interest, the teen-agers were able to relate to me more than expected.

Today, I am not as insecure as I was during my adolescence. Although a lot of personality traits have been changed, I am still a work-in-progress. Change is hard, but it is necessary. My support system consists of a God-fearing, spirit-filled, strong and very independent mother, and friends who help keep me grounded in what I want to do and, by example, remind me of what I don't want to do. The Fruition class was a necessary experience that I will cherish. "What God ordains, He will sustain" is a phrase my mother regularly says to me and my sister. The revisit to Fruition was far greater because it was something God ordained to help in my change from the woman I had become, into the lady by my choice I wanted to be.                     ***Tonya Tyus***

# A Model of Grace and Poise

I was often the awkward-looking girl that felt invisible. I assumed most girls experience this feeling growing up. However, I felt like the only one. I met Johnnie Payne right before I entered this awkward period. She arrived just in time. Johnnie Payne's entrance into my life was indeed divine intervention.

Johnnie invited me to participate in her program, Fruition, when I was 12 years old. This program was to help me realize my full potential as a young lady in various scenarios – from how to answer a phone call, to how to enter/exit a vehicle, or how to handle place settings at the dinner table. However, this experience ended up being so much more.

Later, I began a career as a runway model with the Ebony Fashion Fair. The confidence that bloomed on the inside of me had been planted years prior by the Fruition classes. Through my travels, I have come across many people. Many of those people would compliment me on my grace, elegance, and poise, which I still feel is a lifelong process. However, I was indeed given a gift from Johnnie Payne, the gift of femininity, of owning my womanhood.

Being a female is something that is determined in the womb; being a lady is learned. I have learned how to be a lady from the ultimate lady – Johnnie Payne.

*Andrea C. Norwood*

# TO THE ANGELS ON MY PATH

You have left an indelible mark on my life. God knew exactly who I needed to be touched by in order to begin to fulfill my purpose in Him. From the youngest to the eldest, your strength, courage, talent, and wisdom have made the difference in my life. I truly am convinced that all of you are angels living as people. THANK YOU!

Deloris Bridges, Jackie Christian, Katrina Cazares, Carolyn Harrell, Bunny Wilson, Varetta Heidelberg, Wendy Gladney-Brooks, Crystal Chavez, Marion Williams, Fairlane Williams, Willie Coleman, Helen Patillo, Victoria Roberts, Cheri Brown Costley, Helen Baylor, Dottie Bryant, Latarsha Garland, Binti Harvey, Joyce Geissinger, Kathleen Leighton, Geena Johnson, Deborah Soto, Atiya Henry, Denise Cohen, Laurette Clash, Yvette Thomas, Carolyn Robinson, Rose White, Charlene Vasquez, Phyllis Pugh, Deborah Click, Leah Brown, Edwinna Daniel, Juliette Williams, Mary Crosby, Pansey Washington, Sharmella Ford, Cheron Beard, Benita Love, Edith Silver, Elise Silver, Gladys Smith, Othella Seavers, Grace Spaulding, Tonya Tyus, Andrea Norwood, Nolanda Love, Sister Joanne Laviolette and the Daughters of Charity, Dorothy Scott, Rhonda Mays, Amber Denham, Levetta Washington, Verlander Dixon, Kimala Lewis, Patricia Huggins, Vera Porter, Roberta Williams, Fannie B. Lumbard, and Jaylyn Niccole Weise.

***Johnnie Payne***

# FURTHER GRATITUDE

My spiritual foundation was laid as a child while attending Mount Olive Missionary Baptist Church in Louisville, Kentucky. I will always owe a debt of gratitude to the long-deceased Pastor James Roberts and his wife, Victoria. They held me accountable while training me in the basic principles of faith, and that helped sustain me during the difficult transition from adolescence to adulthood.

When I moved to California in 1971, the pastoral mantel for my training was passed, so to speak, to the late Bishop James Edward Henry, who believed in me and encouraged me to write the vision and make it plain concerning classes for girls. I am thankful that he saw in me something I did not know existed.

The late Pastor Carolyn Harrell was a strong motivating force in my life. She had a way of propelling anyone who spent time with her to the next level. That was truly one of her God-given talents. She commanded an example of excellence that was exemplified in everything she did. Carolyn Harrell will always be my shero.

Lastly, I thank my current Pastor, Bishop Milton Morris White Sr. and First Lady Patricia White, a man and woman of vision whom I admire and respect. Thank you both for pressing me to higher heights and deeper depths, all for the purpose of accomplishing great things for the Kingdom.

Lovingly,

*Johnnie Payne*

*A heartfelt thank you to*

*Stanley O. Williford*

*and*

**Vision**
**PUBLISHING**
Carson, California

*a company of integrity and excellence.*

# *Look for these upcoming books from Johnnie Payne and Fruition Ministries:*

\*\* A Lady by Choice Journal

\*\*A Christian Counselor's Guide to Aiding Troubled Teens

\* \* \* \* \* \* \* \* \* \* \* \* \* \* \* \* \* \* \* \* \* \* \*

*If you would like to have information regarding A Lady by Choice retreats for teen-age girls, please contact us through our website at* **www.fruitionministries.com**.

# ABOUT THE AUTHOR

Johnnie Denise Payne is the founder of Fruition Ministries. Her workshops and seminars assist young ladies in their development from adolescence to womanhood. She has taught personal development classes in the Pasadena and Los Angeles school systems, and has worked as a supervising counselor in a treatment center for severely emotionally disturbed girls for the past ten years.

As a true woman of God, equipped and anointed to do the work she has been called to, Johnnie has learned virtually every pitfall that young ladies fall into, and she is zealous about training them up in the way they should go. This, along with her God-given gift for hearing the heart of troubled young ladies, aids her well in doing what she has been called to do.

Johnnie is a representative of God's Word in action, an older woman sowing into the lives of young women. This is the ministerial calling she answered more than twenty years ago.

A native of Louisville, Kentucky, she presently resides in Pasadena, California, with her husband, Don. They have enjoyed twenty-one years of marriage and have one son, Jeremiah, and a granddaughter, Jaylyn Niccole.